McGraw-Hill
Mathematics

Transition Handbook

Bridge the Gaps!

What Do I Need to Know?

Skill Builder

Challenge

1

McGraw-Hill School Division

New York   Farmington

McGraw-Hill School Division

A Division of The McGraw-Hill Companies

Copyright © McGraw-Hill School Division,
a Division of the Educational and Professional Publishing Group of The McGraw-Hill Companies, Inc.
All rights reserved.

McGraw-Hill School Division
Two Penn Plaza
New York, New York 10121-2298

Printed in the United States of America

ISBN 0-02-100138-3 / 1

1 2 3 4 5 6 7 8 9 066 05 04 03 02 01 00

GRADE 1 Contents

More or Fewer

Learn

What Can I Do? I want to find which has more.

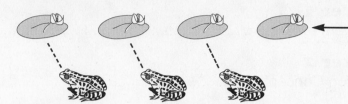

Match.

Find the one with **more.**

There are more .

There are fewer .

Try It • Match. Circle the one that has more.

1.

more

more

2.

more

more

Name_____

Power Practice

Match. Circle the one that has more.

3.    more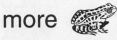

    more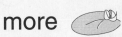

4.   more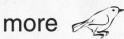

      more

5.   more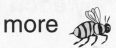

 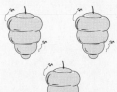   more

Match. Circle the one that has fewer.

6.   fewer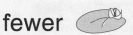

      fewer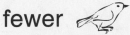

7.   fewer

      fewer

Copy a Pattern

Learn

What Can I Do?
I want to copy
a pattern.

Look for chunks.

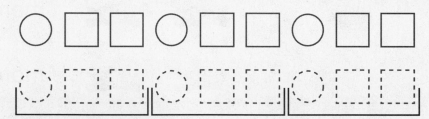

Copy each chunk.

Try It • Copy each pattern.

1. ▢ ◯ ◯ ▢ ◯ ▢ ◯

_____

2. ◯ ◯ ◯ ◯ ▢ ◯ ◯ ◯ ▢ ◯ ◯ ◯ ▢

_____

Power Practice • Copy each pattern.

3. ◯ △ △ ◯ △ ◯ △ _____

4. ◯ ▢ △ ◯ ▢ △ ◯ ▢ △ _____

Extend a Pattern

Learn

What Can I Do?
I want to draw the next shape in a pattern.

Look for chunks.

Match. Draw the missing shape.

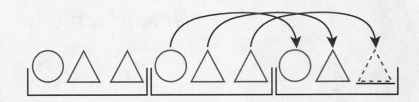

Try It • **Draw what could be the next shape in the pattern.**

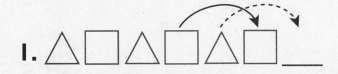

1. △ □ △ □ △ □ ___

2. △ △ △ ○ ○ ○ △ △ ○ ○ △ △ ___

Power Practice • **Draw what could be the next shape in the pattern.**

3. ○ □ ○ ○ □ ○ ○ □ ○ ○ □ ○ ___

4. □ ○ ○ □ ○ ○ □ ○ ___

5. △ ○ ○ □ △ ○ ○ □ △ ○ ___

Numbers to 5

Learn

Count one number for each picture.

   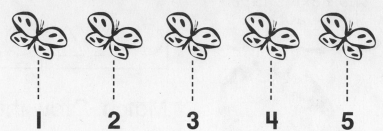

| 1 | 2 | 3 | 4 | 5 |

Write how many.

5

Try It • Count. Write how many.

1.

2

2.

_____

3.

_____

4.

_____

Power Practice • Count. Write how many.

5.

_ _ _ _

6.

_ _ _ _

7.

_ _ _ _

8.

_ _ _ _

9.

_ _ _ _

10.

_ _ _ _

Before, After, Between

Learn

Look left to find the one **before**.

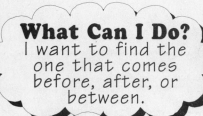

is before .

Look right to find the one **after**.

is after .

Look left and right to find the one **between**.

is between and .

Name_____

1. before

2. after

Power Practice • Circle the one that comes before, after, or between.

3. before

4. after

5. between  and

6. between and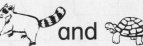

© McGraw-Hill School Division

Name_____

Pattern Maze

This pattern repeats in chunks of 4.

○ △ □ ☆ ○ △ □ ☆ ○ △ □ ☆

Follow the pattern. Go right, left, or down. Color the next shape in the pattern. Find the way to the end.

START

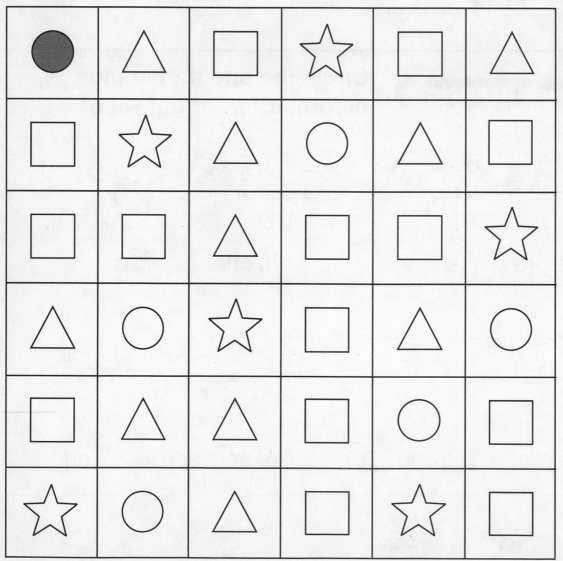

END

Name_____

Pattern Necklaces

Each 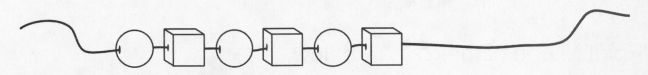 has a pattern. Find the pattern. Count the beads. Draw what could be the rest of the beads for each 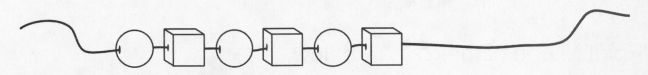 .

1. This 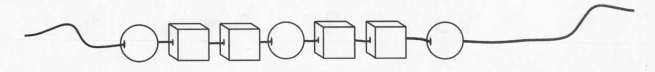 needs 10 beads in all.

2. This 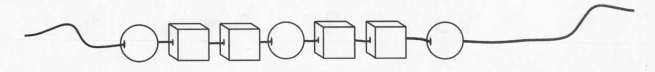 needs 9 beads in all.

3. This 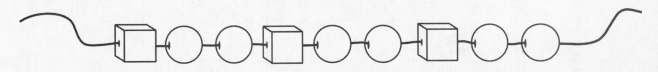 needs 10 beads in all.

4. This  needs 9 beads in all.

Name_____

Race Around the Pond

Play with a partner.

Put your  on  .

Take turns.

Close your eyes.

Point to one of the ⟦• • •⟧ below.

Move that number of spaces on the  .

•	two	2	• • •	three
four	1	 🐸	one	⁙ (5 dots)
3	 🐸🐸🐸	• •	4	five
• • • •	 🐸🐸🐸🐸	5	 🐸🐸	 🐸🐸🐸🐸

Name_____

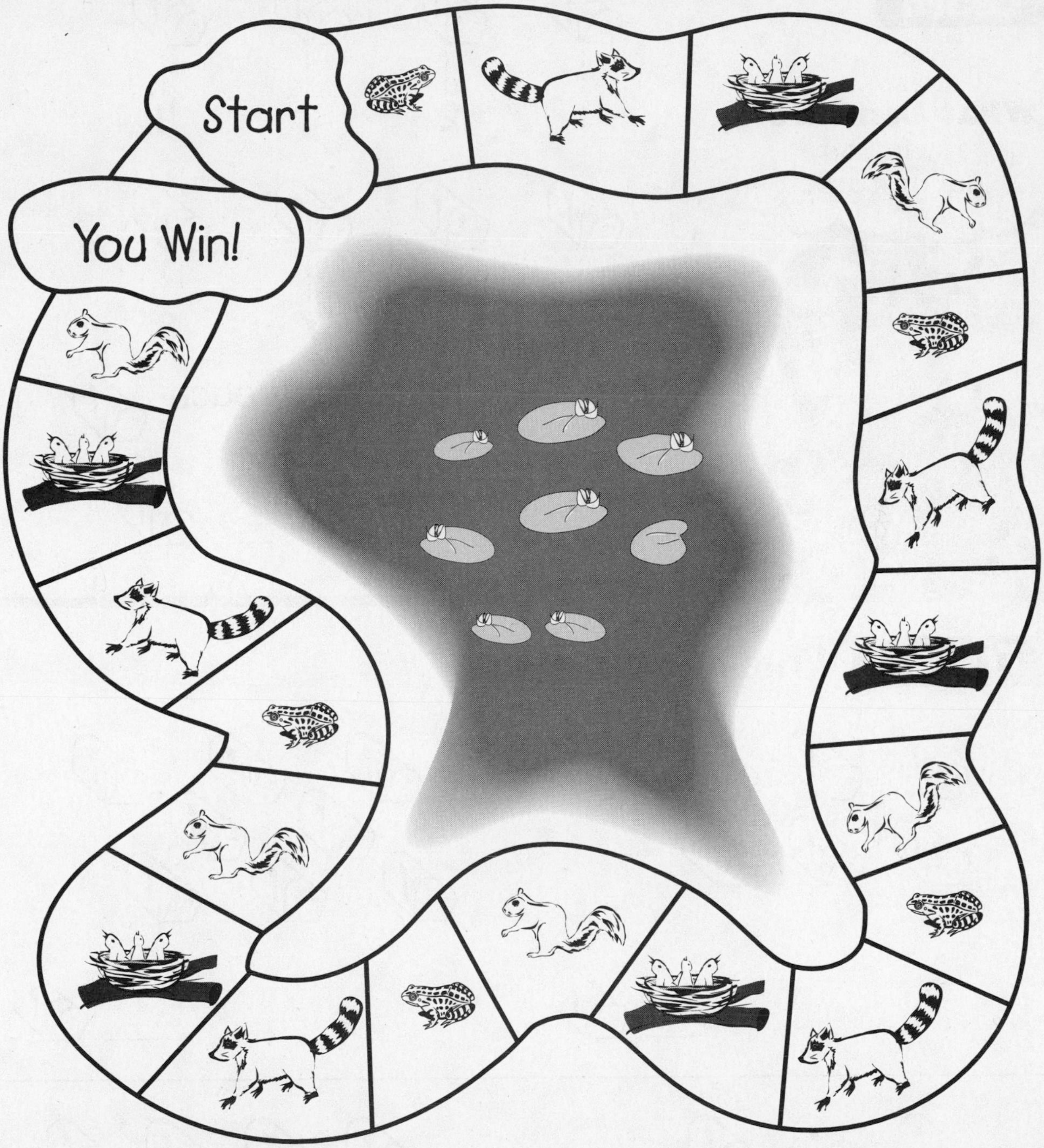

Start

You Win!

How many 🐸 ? ____   How many 🦝 ? ____

How many 🪹 ? ____   How many 🐿️ ? ____

Numbers to 8

Learn

What Can I Do?
I want to count to 8.

1   2   3   4

5   6   7   8

Count one number for each .

Write how many. 8

Try It • Write how many.

1.

6

2.

___

3.

___

4.

___

Power Practice • Write how many.

5. 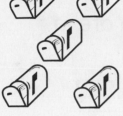 _____

6.   _____

7. 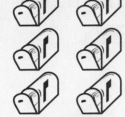 _____

8. 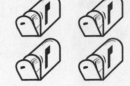 _____

9.  _____

10. _____

11.   _____

12. 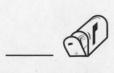 _____

Compare Numbers

Learn

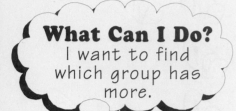

What Can I Do?
I want to find which group has more.

Count how many there are in each group.

 6

 5

Find the group that has more.

6 🚌 are more than 5 🚌 .

Try It • Write how many.
Circle the group that has more.

1.  5 🚌

🚌🚌🚌🚌🚌🚌🚌 7 🚌

---

2. 🚌🚌🚌🚌   🚌🚌🚌

🚌🚌🚌🚌   🚌🚌🚌

_____    _____

Name_____

3. ____ ____

4. ____ ____

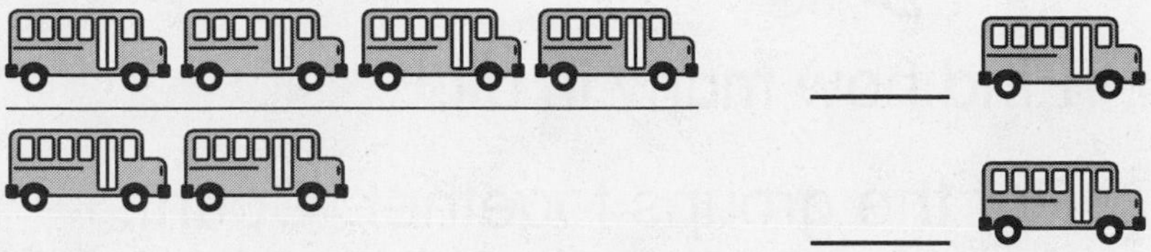

5. ____ ____

6. ____ ____

7. ____ ____

Concept of Addition

 **Learn**

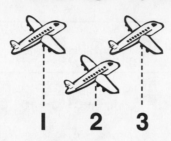

 **What Can I Do?**
I want to count how many in all.

Find how many in all.

Put the groups together. Count.

1   **2**   **3**   **4**

3 and 1 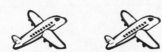 are 4 in all.

Try It • Write how many  in all.

1.

2 and 1 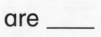 are **3** in all.

2.

2 and 2 are ____ in all.

3.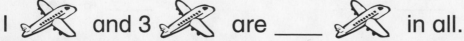

1 and 3 ____ are ____ in all.

Name_____

Power Practice • Write how many in all.

4.      _____  in all.

5.      _____  in all.

6.      _____  in all.

7.      _____  in all.

8.      _____  in all.

9.      _____  in all.

10.   _____ in all.

11.    _____ in all.

Same Numbers

Learn

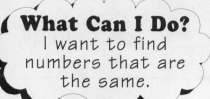

What Can I Do?
I want to find
numbers that are
the same.

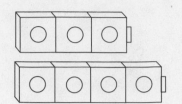

Count each group.

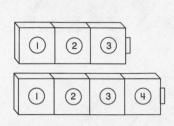 

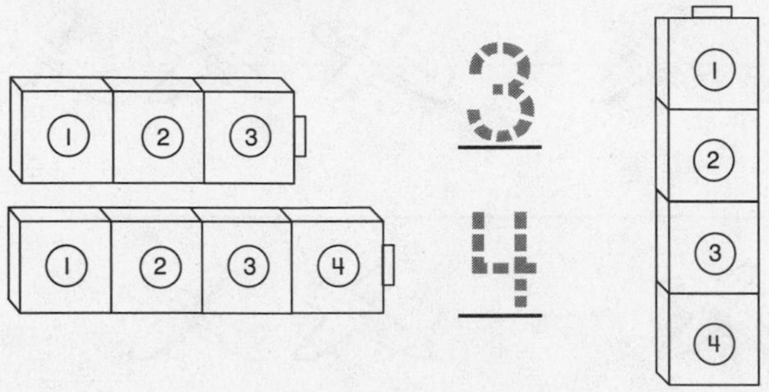

Find numbers that are the same.

4 = 4

Try It • Write how many.
Circle numbers that are the same.

1.

  3

2.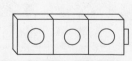

_____   _____   _____

Power Practice
• Write how many.
Circle numbers that are the same.

3.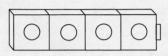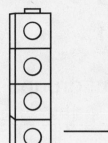

_____   _____   _____

4.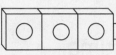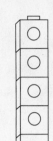

_____   _____   _____

5.

_____   _____   _____

6.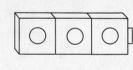

_____   _____   _____

7.

_____   _____   _____

Add Sums to 5

Learn

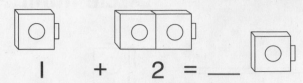

1 + 2 = ___

What Can I Do?
I want to add.

Put groups together.

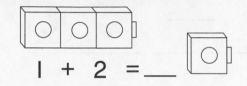

1 + 2 = ___

Count to find the sums.

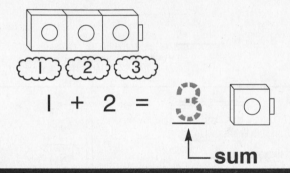

1 + 2 = **3**

↑
sum

Try It • Add. Write each sum.

1.

2 + 2 = **4**

2.

3 + 2 = ___

3.

1 + 1 = ___

Name_____

Power Practice • Add. Write each sum.

4.

     2   +   2   = __

5.

     3   +   1   = __

6.

     1   +   4   = __

7.

     2   +   3   = __

8.

     1   +   3   = __

9.

     4   +   1   = __

10.

     2   +   2   = __

Name_____

Addition Town

Use a ⊂⊃ and a ✏ .

Make the spinners below.

Take turns with a partner.

Player 1 uses ◖red◗.

Player 2 uses ◖blue◗.

Spin both and ⬤.

Add the numbers.

Color the sum on the ▦.

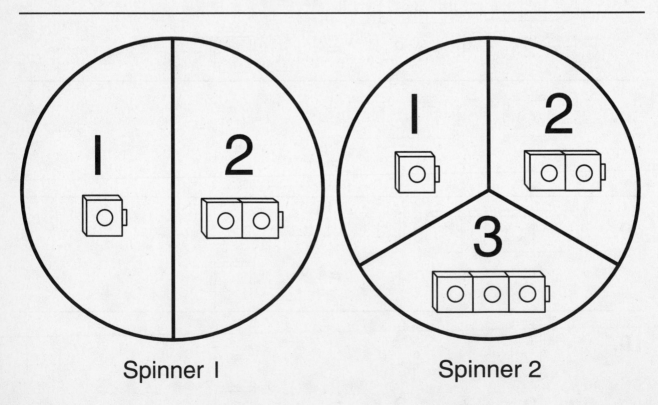

Spinner 1   Spinner 2

Name_____

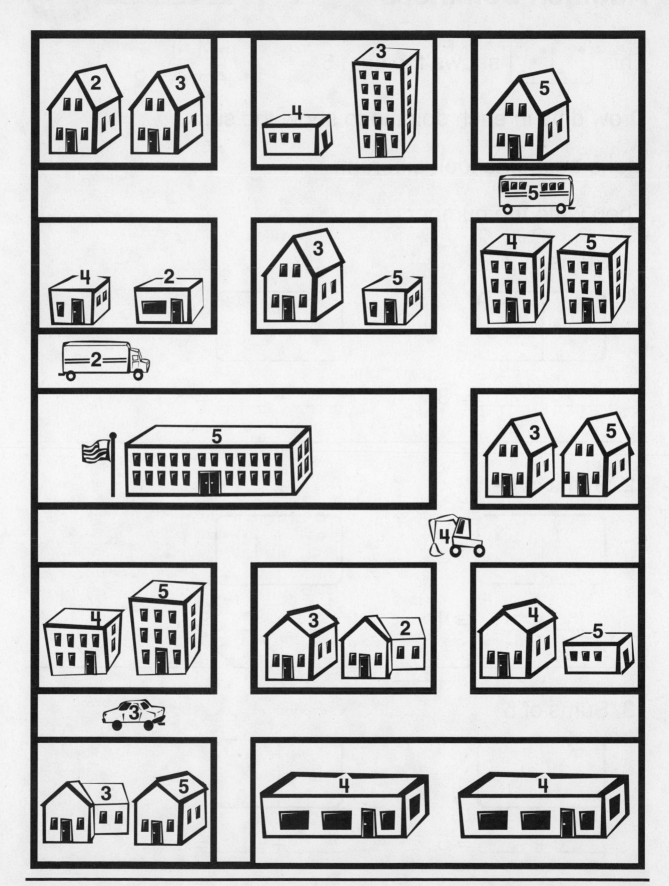

Addition Dominoes

This 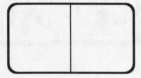 shows the sum 5.

$2 + 3 = 5$

Draw dots in each domino to show the sum.

Make each one look different.

Then write the numbers.

1. Sums of 3

_____ + _____ = 3   _____ + _____ = 3

2. Sums of 4

   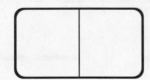

_____ + _____ = 4   _____ + _____ = 4

3. Sums of 5

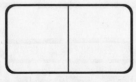   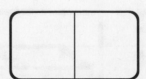

_____ + _____ = 5   _____ + _____ = 5

Name_____

More Addition Dominoes

Draw 2 different dominoes for each sum.

Each space can have only 6 or fewer dots.

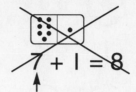

6 + 2 = 8

~~7 + 1 = 8~~

7 is more than 6.

---

1. Sums of 6

____ + ____ = 6   ____ + ____ = 6

---

2. Sums of 7

____ + ____ = 7   ____ + ____ = 7

---

3. Sums of 8

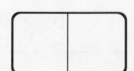

____ + ____ = 8   ____ + ____ = 8

© McGraw-Hill School Division

Grade 1, Chapter 2, Cluster B 27

Numbers to 12

Learn

What Can I Do?
I want to count
to 12.

Count one number for each .

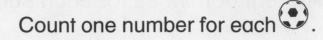

1   2   3   4   5   6

7   8   9   10   11   12

Write how many.

__12__

Try It • **Count. Write how many.**

1.
1   2   3   4   5   6   7   _8_   _9_   _9_

2.
     ___

3.
       ___

Name_____

4.

_____

5.

_____

6.

_____

7.

_____

8.

_____

9.

_____

10.

_____

Order Numbers to 12

Learn

Count to find the missing number.

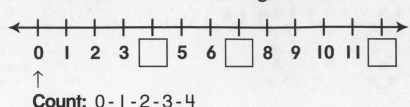

Count: 0-1-2-3-4

Count to find the next missing number.

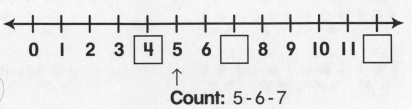

What Can I Do?
I want to put numbers in order.

Count: 5-6-7

Count to find the last missing number.

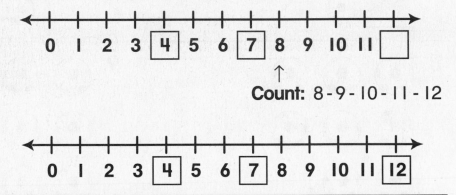

Count: 8-9-10-11-12

Try It • **Write the number that goes in each box.**

1.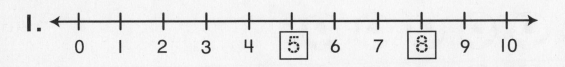

2.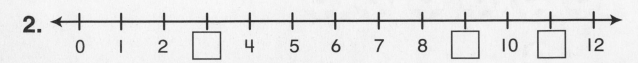

Name_____

Power Practice • Write the number that goes in each box.

3.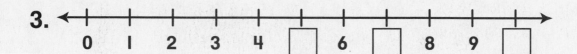

0 1 2 3 4 ☐ 6 ☐ 8 9 ☐

4.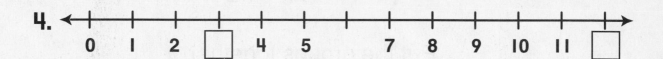

0 1 2 ☐ 4 5 7 8 9 10 11 ☐

5.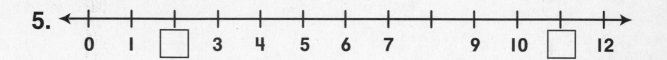

0 1 ☐ 3 4 5 6 7 9 10 ☐ 12

6.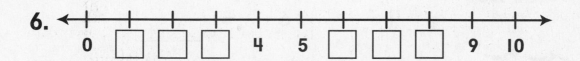

0 ☐ ☐ ☐ 4 5 ☐ ☐ ☐ 9 10

7.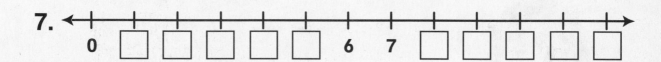

0 ☐ ☐ ☐ ☐ ☐ 6 7 ☐ ☐ ☐ ☐ ☐

Write the numbers in order.

8. | 3 | 2 |
   |---|---|
   | 4 | 1 |

   _1_ _2_ _3_ _4_

9. | 9 | 11 |
   |---|----|
   | 12 | 10 |

   _9_ ___ ___ ___

Name ____________________________________

CHAPTER 3 Skill Builder

Add Sums to 10

Learn

How many in all?

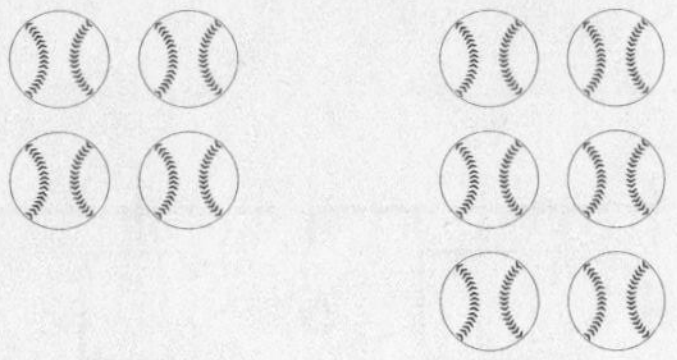

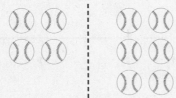

4 + 6 = ____

Put the groups together.

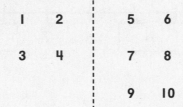

4 + 6 = ____

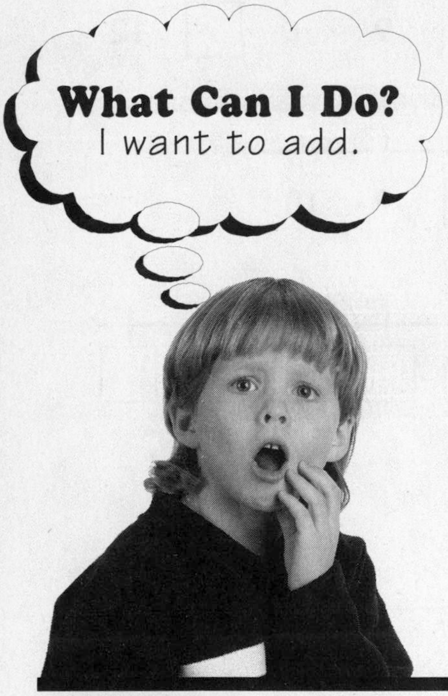

What Can I Do?
I want to add.

Count on. Write how many in all.

1 2	5 6
3 4	7 8
	9 10

4 + 6 = ____

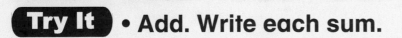

Try It • **Add. Write each sum.**

1.

6 + 3 = ____

2. ⚾⚾⚾⚾⚾⚾   ⚾⚾⚾⚾⚾

$$5 \quad + \quad 5 \quad = \quad \underline{\quad} \quad ⚾$$

3. 4 ⚾⚾⚾⚾⚾
   + 1 ⚾⚾

4. 3 ⚾⚾⚾⚾⚾
   + 3 ⚾⚾⚾⚾⚾

Power Practice • Add. Write each sum.

5. ⚾⚾⚾⚾⚾ ⚾⚾
⚾⚾⚾⚾⚾

$$8 \quad + \quad 1 \quad = \quad \underline{\quad}$$

6. ⚾⚾⚾⚾ ⚾⚾⚾⚾
⚾⚾

$$5 \quad + \quad 3 \quad = \quad \underline{\quad}$$

7. ⚾⚾ ⚾⚾⚾⚾⚾
⚾⚾⚾⚾⚾

$$2 \quad + \quad 7 \quad = \quad \underline{\quad}$$

8. ⚾⚾⚾⚾⚾ ⚾⚾
⚾⚾⚾⚾⚾
⚾⚾⚾⚾

$$9 \quad + \quad 1 \quad = \quad \underline{\quad}$$

9. 4 ⚾⚾⚾⚾⚾
   + 4 ⚾⚾⚾⚾⚾

10. 5 ⚾⚾⚾⚾⚾⚾⚾
    + 2 ⚾⚾⚾

11. 7 + 3 = _____

12. 4 + 5 = _____

13. 6
    + 2

14. 3
    + 4

15. 6
    + 4

16. 7
    + 2

Patterns

Learn

What Can I Do?
I want to write what comes next in a pattern.

4 5 4 5 4 5 4 5 4 ___

Find the chunks that repeat.

4 5 | 4 5 | 4 5 | 4 5 | 4 ___

Write the number that could come next.

4 5 | 4 5 | 4 5 | 4 5 | 4 _5_

Try It • **Write the number that could come next in the pattern.**

1. 3 4 5 | 3 4 5 | 3 4 5 | 3 4 ___

2. 7 8 7 8 7 8 7 8 7 ___

3. 7 8 9 7 8 9 7 8 9 7 8 ___

4. 3 3 6 3 3 6 3 3 6 3 3 6 ___

Power Practice • Write the number that could come next in the pattern.

5. 8 9 8 9 8 9 8 9 8 ____

_____

6. 2 2 4 2 2 4 2 2 4 2 2 ____

_____

7. 2 3 5 2 3 5 2 3 5 2 3 ____

_____

8. 6 7 8 6 7 8 6 7 8 6 7 8 ____

_____

9. 4 4 8 4 4 8 4 4 8 ____

_____

10. 5 1 6 5 1 6 5 1 6 5 1 ____

_____

11. 7 2 9 7 2 9 7 2 9 7 2 ____

_____

12. 4 5 9 4 5 9 4 5 9 4 5 ____

_____

13. 3 5 8 3 5 8 3 5 8 ____

_____

Greatest Sum Game

Play with a partner.

Use a ⊂⊃ and a ✏ HB .

Make the spinner below.

To play:

Take turns.

Spin the spinner.

On the game board try to make the greatest sum you can.

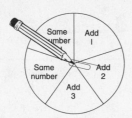

Player 1 Game 1	Player 2 Game 1
0 + ____ = ____	0 + ____ = ____
1 + ____ = ____	1 + ____ = ____
2 + ____ = ____	2 + ____ = ____
3 + ____ = ____	3 + ____ = ____
4 + ____ = ____	4 + ____ = ____
Player 1 Game 2	Player 2 Game 2
0 + ____ = ____	0 + ____ = ____
1 + ____ = ____	1 + ____ = ____
2 + ____ = ____	2 + ____ = ____
3 + ____ = ____	3 + ____ = ____
4 + ____ = ____	4 + ____ = ____

At the end of the game, the player with the greatest sum wins.

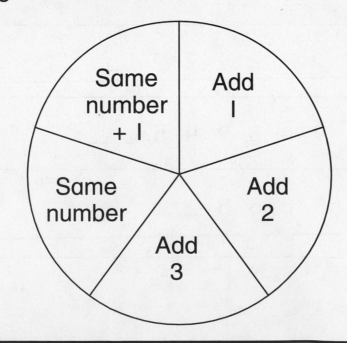

Greatest Sum Game

Player 1	Player 2
Game 1	**Game 1**

Player 1
Game 1

0 + _____ = _____

1 + _____ = _____

2 + _____ = _____

3 + _____ = _____

4 + _____ = _____

Player 2
Game 1

0 + _____ = _____

1 + _____ = _____

2 + _____ = _____

3 + _____ = _____

4 + _____ = _____

Player 1
Game 2

0 + _____ = _____

1 + _____ = _____

2 + _____ = _____

3 + _____ = _____

4 + _____ = _____

Player 2
Game 2

0 + _____ = _____

1 + _____ = _____

2 + _____ = _____

3 + _____ = _____

4 + _____ = _____

CHALLENGE **CHAPTER** **3**

Addition Concentration

Copy the cards.

Cut them out.

Mix them up.

Turn them face down.

Play with a partner.

		$2 + 2$	
	$3 + 1$		

To play:

Take turns.

Turn over 2 cards.

Keep cards with the same sum.

Turn over cards that don't have the same sum.

The player with the most cards wins.

$3 + 1$	$2 + 2$	$2 + 3$
$4 + 1$	$3 + 3$	$4 + 2$
$5 + 2$	$6 + 1$	$4 + 4$

5 + 3	8 + 1	7 + 2
5 + 5	8 + 2	5 + 1
6 + 0	4 + 3	7 + 0
2 + 6	7 + 1	6 + 3
4 + 5	7 + 3	9 + 1

Name _____

Numbers to 8

Learn

Count one number for each .

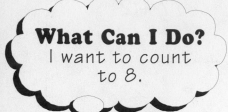

What Can I Do?
I want to count to 8.

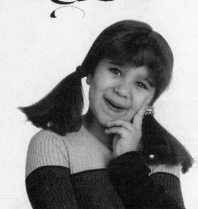

Write how many.

8

Try It • Write how many.

1.

4

2.

____

Power Practice • Write how many.

3.

____

4.

____

More or Fewer

Learn

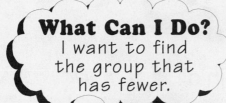

What Can I Do? I want to find the group that has fewer.

Match. Write how many of each.

5
3

Find the group that has **fewer**. **Fewer** means not as many.

3  is fewer than 5  .

Try It • Write how many.
Circle the group that has fewer.

1.  6   (3)

2.  _____   _____

Power Practice • Write how many.
Circle the group that has fewer.

3. _____   _____

4. _____   _____

Add Sums to 8.

Learn

Find how many in all.

Put the groups together.

4 + 2 = __6__

Count on to find how many in all.

4   5   6

Write the sum.

4 + 2 = __6__

What Can I Do?
I want to add sums to 8.

Try It • Add. Write each sum.

1.

3 + 1 = __4__

2.

4 + 3 = ___

3.   2
    + 1

4.   3
    + 2

Power Practice • Add. Write each sum.

5.

5 + 1 = _____

6.

6 + 2 = _____

7.   3
    + 4

8.   5
    + 3

9. 6 + 1 = _____

10. 5 + 2 = _____

11. 2 + 6 = _____

12. 3 + 1 = _____

13. 4 + 4 = _____

14. 7 + 1 = _____

15.   1
     + 4

16.   8
     + 0

17.   3
     + 3

18.   2
     + 4

19.   1
     + 6

20.   2
     + 2

21.   2
     + 5

22.   2
     + 3

Same Numbers

Learn

Count each group.
Write how many.

____ ____ ____
4   2   4

Circle the numbers that are the same.

What Can I Do?
I want to find
the same
numbers.

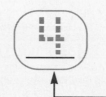

(4)   2   (4)

↑ ———— same ———— ↑

Try It • Write how many.
Circle the numbers that are the same.

1.  (3)

 (3)

 4

2.   ____

    ____

    ____

Power Practice • Write how many. Circle the numbers that are the same.

3.  ____

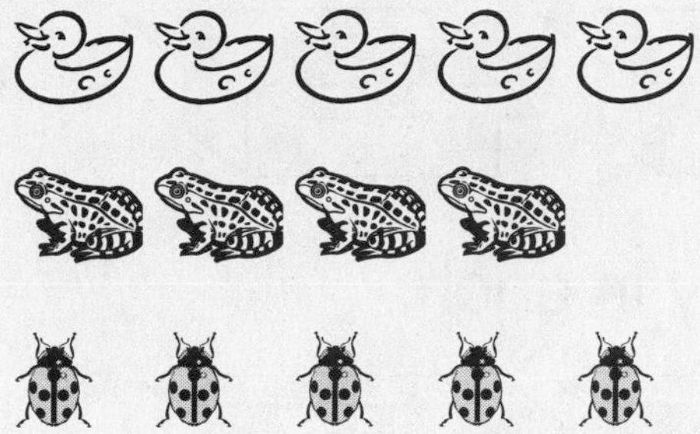

    ____

    ____

4.

   ____   ____   ____

5.

   ____   ____   ____

6.

   ____   ____   ____

Add Zero

Learn

How many 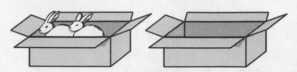 in all?

Write how many in each.

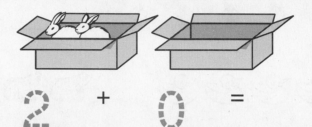

$$2 + 0 = \underline{}$$

Put the groups together. Count.

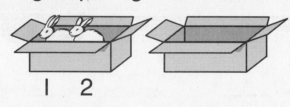

   1   2

Write how many in all.

$$2 + 0 = \underline{2}$$

What Can I Do?
I want to add zero to a number.

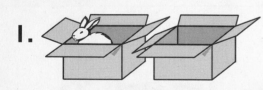

Try It • Add. Write each sum.

1.

$$1 + 0 = \underline{1}$$

2.

$$4 + 0 = \underline{}$$

3. $\begin{array}{r} 3 \\ + 0 \\ \hline \end{array}$

4. $\begin{array}{r} 2 \\ + 0 \\ \hline \end{array}$

Name_____

5.

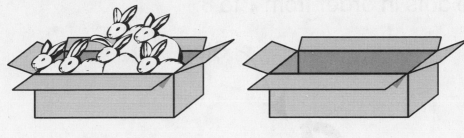

$6 + 0 = $____

6.

$8 + 0 = $____

7. 5
     + 0

8. 7
     + 0

9. $2 + 0 = $____

10. $7 + 0 = $____

11. $5 + 0 = $____

12. $3 + 0 = $____

13. 4
      + 0

14. 0
      + 0

15. 6
      + 0

16. 1
      + 0

Addition Dot-to-Dot

Write each sum.

Connect the dots in order from 1 to 8.

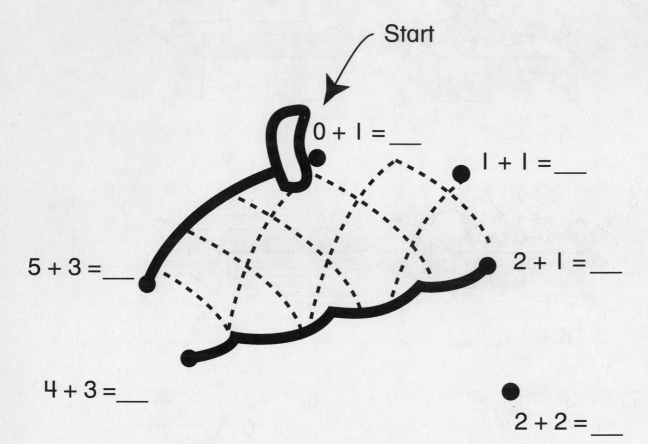

Start

0 + 1 = ___

1 + 1 = ___

5 + 3 = ___

2 + 1 = ___

4 + 3 = ___

2 + 2 = ___

3 + 3 = ___

5 + 0 = ___

Number Shapes

Here are three ways to show 5.

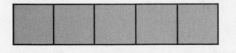 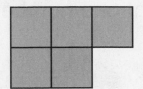 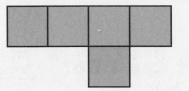

Shade the squares to show each number.

Show three different ways for each number.

1. Show 6.

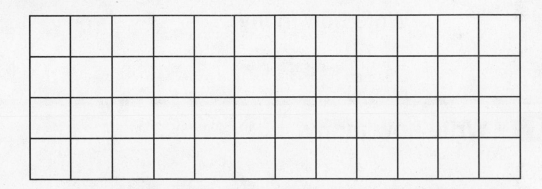

2. Show 8.

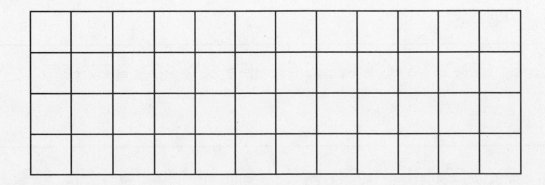

Name________________________________

Numbers to 12

Learn

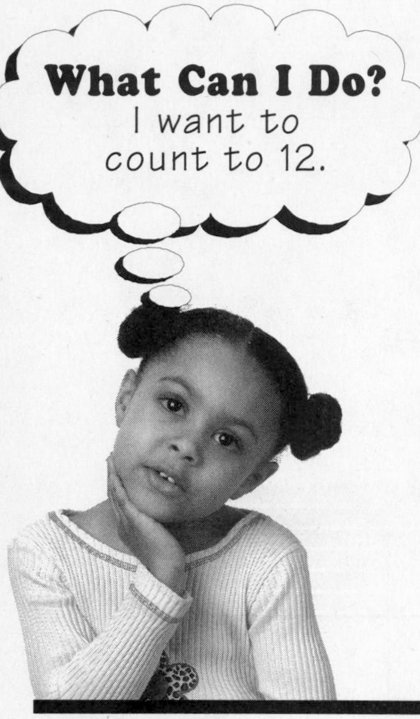

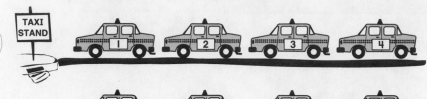

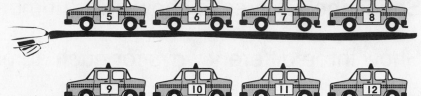

What Can I Do?
I want to count to 12.

Count one number for each.

TAXI STAND
1
2
3
4
5
6
7
8
9
10
11
12

Write how many.

12

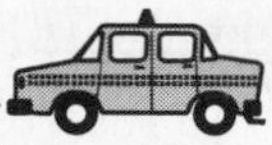

Try It • Write how many.

1.

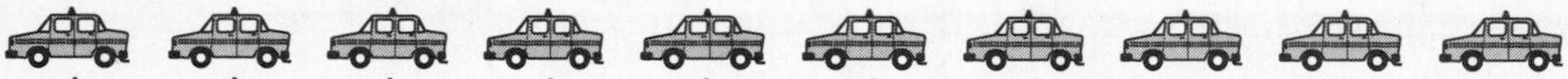

1 2 3 4 5 [6] [7] [8] [9] [10]

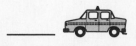

10

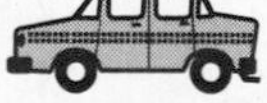

2.

____

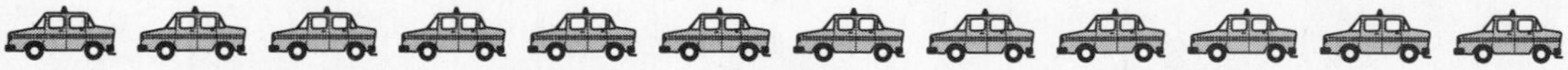

3.

____

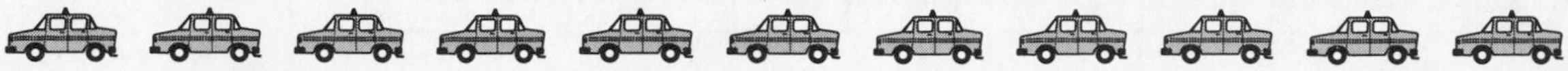

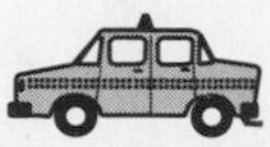

Name____________________________________

Power Practice • **Write how many.**

4.

____

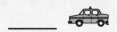

5.

____

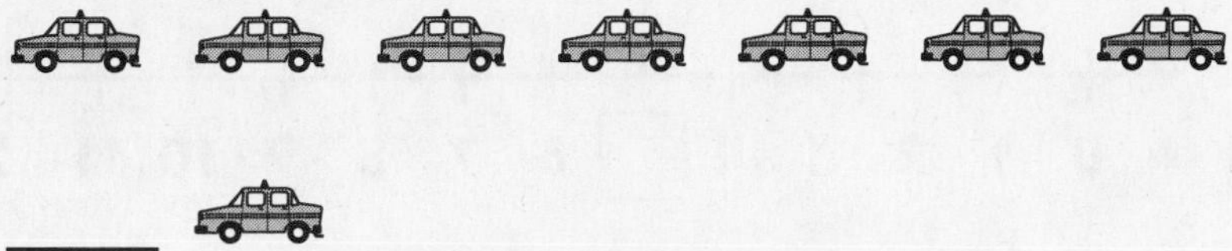

6.

____

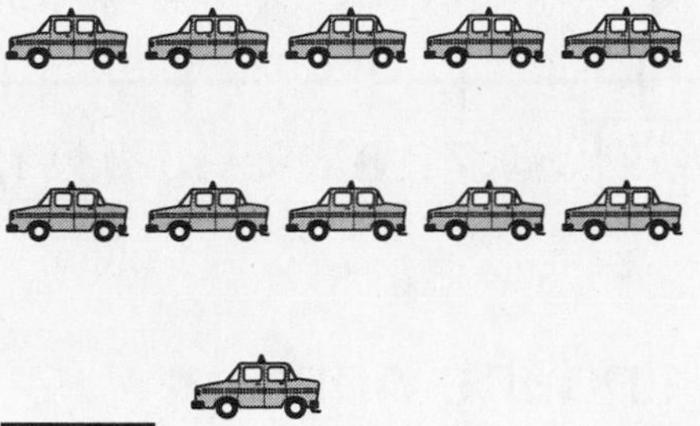

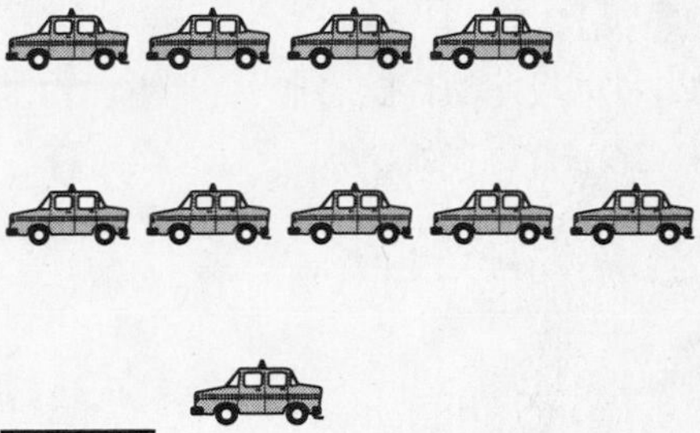

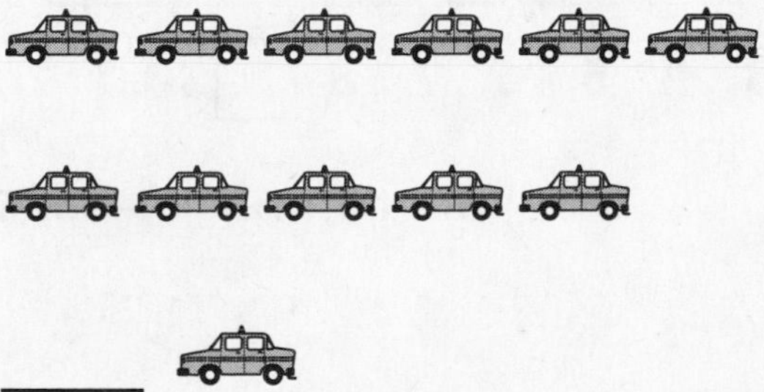

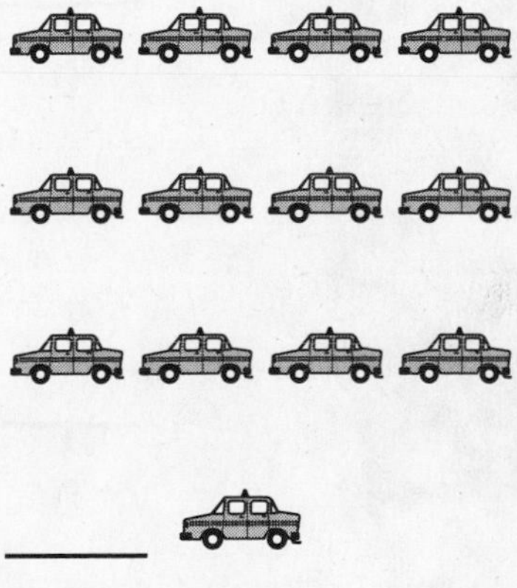

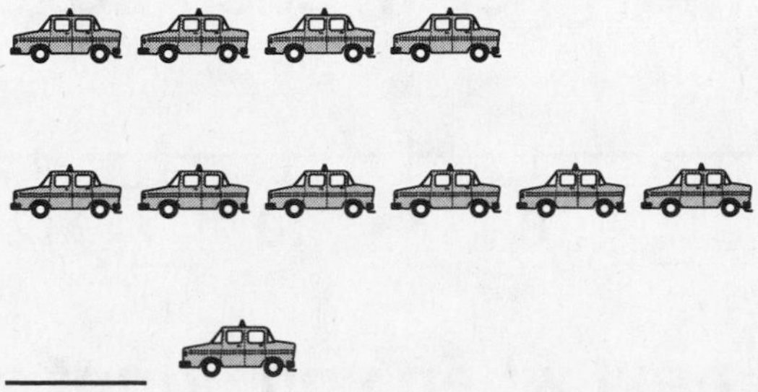

7.

____

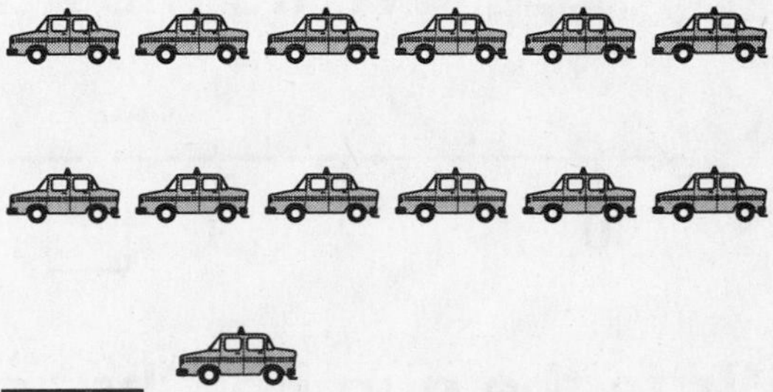

8.

____

9.

____

10.

____

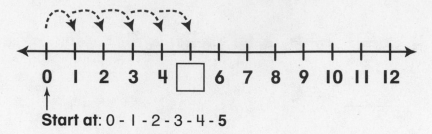

Order Numbers to 12

Learn

Count on to find the number.

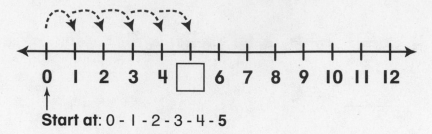

Start at: 0 - 1 - 2 - 3 - 4 - 5

What Can I Do?
I want to count on and count back.

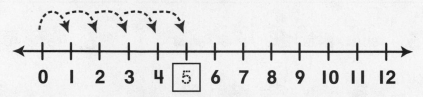

Count back to find the number.

Start at: 12 - 11 - 10 - 9

Try It • **Write the number that goes in each box.**

1.

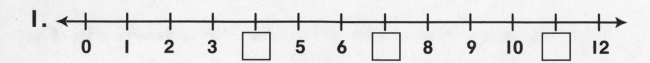

Write the number that comes next when you count.

2. 4, 5, 6, 7, _____   **3.** 7, 6, 5, 4, _____

Name_____

4.

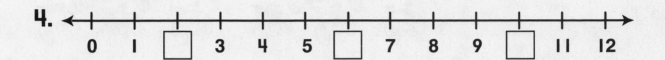

0 1 ☐ 3 4 5 ☐ 7 8 9 ☐ 11 12

5.

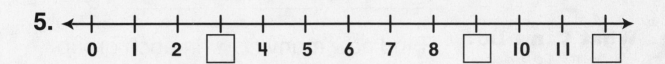

0 1 2 ☐ 4 5 6 7 8 ☐ 10 11 ☐

6.

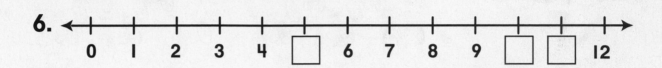

0 1 2 3 4 ☐ 6 7 8 9 ☐ ☐ 12

Write the number that comes next when you count on or count back.

7. 1, 2, 3, 4, 5, ____

8. 7, 8, 9, 10, 11, ____

9. 3, 4, 5, 6, 7, ____

10. 6, 5, 4, 3, 2, ____

11. 10, 9, 8, 7, ____

12. 12, 11, 10, 9, ____

Add Sums to 12

Learn

Find how many  in all.

_____ + _____ = _____

What Can I Do?
I want to add.

Find how many  in each group.

__5__ + __5__ = _____

Add doubles

__5__ + __5__ = _____

Try It • Add. Write each sum.

1.

   4 + 4 = ____

2.   5
   + 6

---

3. 6 + 6 = ____

4.   4
   + 5

Name_____

Power Practice • Add. Write each sum.

5.

$9 + 1 =$ _____

6.

$3 + 3 =$ _____

---

7. $\begin{array}{r} 8 \\ + 3 \\ \hline \end{array}$

8. $\begin{array}{r} 7 \\ + 2 \\ \hline \end{array}$

---

9. $6 + 5 =$ _____

10. $8 + 2 =$ _____

11. $2 + 2 =$ _____

12. $7 + 5 =$ _____

13. $6 + 1 =$ _____

14. $6 + 6 =$ _____

---

15. $\begin{array}{r} 9 \\ + 2 \\ \hline \end{array}$

16. $\begin{array}{r} 6 \\ + 3 \\ \hline \end{array}$

17. $\begin{array}{r} 4 \\ + 2 \\ \hline \end{array}$

18. $\begin{array}{r} 8 \\ + 4 \\ \hline \end{array}$

Subtraction

Learn

5 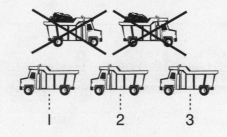 take away 2 is ____ left.

Cross out to find out how many are left.

I   2   3

3 are left.

5 − 2 = **3** left.

Try It • Write how many are left.

I.

3 − 1 = **2** left.

2.

5 − 3 = ____ left.

Name_____

3.

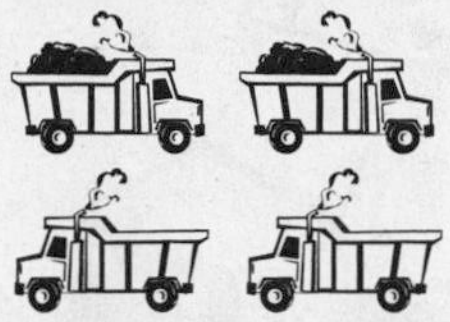

4 🚚 − 2 🚚 = _____ 🚚 left.

4.

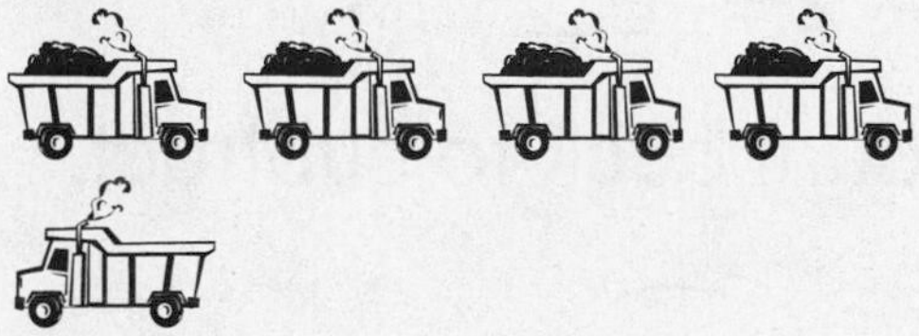

5 🚚 − 4 🚚 = _____ 🚚 left.

5.

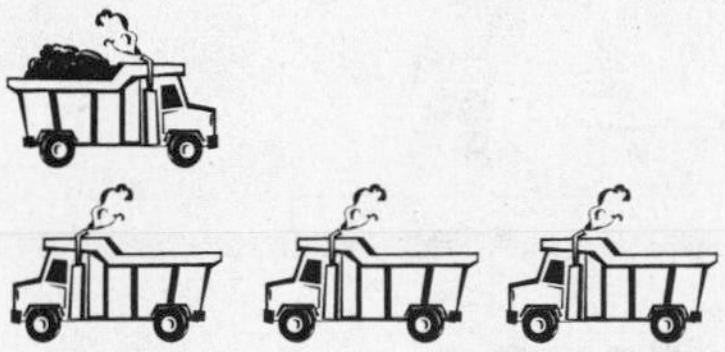

4 🚚 − 1 🚚 = _____ 🚚 left.

6.

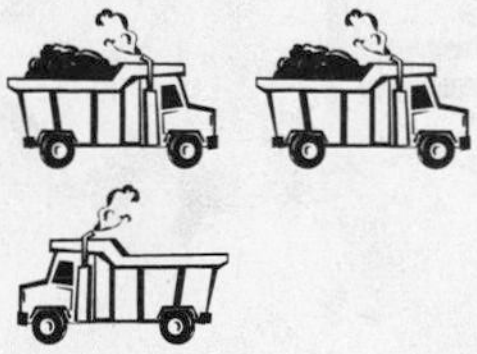

3 🚚 − 2 🚚 = _____ 🚚 left.

7.

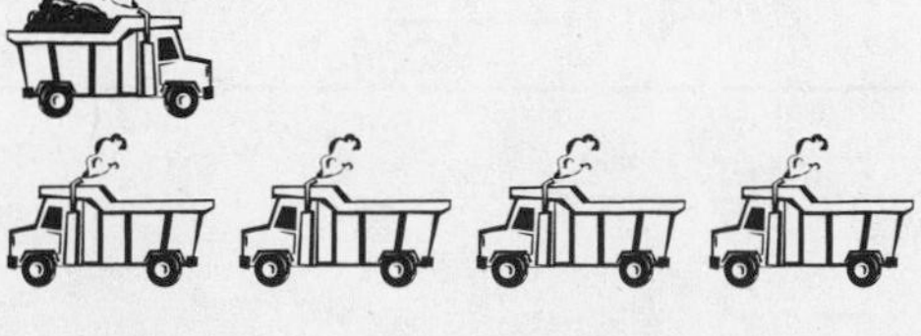

5 🚚 − 1 🚚 = _____ 🚚 left.

Subtract from 8

Learn

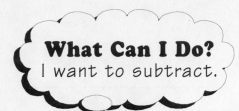

What Can I Do?
I want to subtract.

$7 - 2 =$ ____

Count back to subtract.

7   6   5

$7 - 2 =$ 5

Try It • **Subtract. Write each difference.**

1.

$7 - 1 =$ 6

2.   6
   -2

---

3. $5 - 1 =$ ____

4. $8 - 2 =$ ____

---

5.   2
   -1

6.   4
   -2

Power Practice • Subtract. Write each difference.

7.

$6 - 3 =$ _____

8.

$4 - 1 =$ _____

9. $\begin{array}{r} 8 \\ -\ 4 \\ \hline \end{array}$

10. $\begin{array}{r} 6 \\ -\ 1 \\ \hline \end{array}$

11. $7 - 3 =$ _____

12. $6 - 4 =$ _____

13. $3 - 1 =$ _____

14. $5 - 2 =$ _____

15. $\begin{array}{r} 7 \\ -\ 4 \\ \hline \end{array}$

16. $\begin{array}{r} 8 \\ -\ 6 \\ \hline \end{array}$

17. $\begin{array}{r} 5 \\ -\ 4 \\ \hline \end{array}$

18. $\begin{array}{r} 7 \\ -\ 6 \\ \hline \end{array}$

Parking Lot Count

Color 8 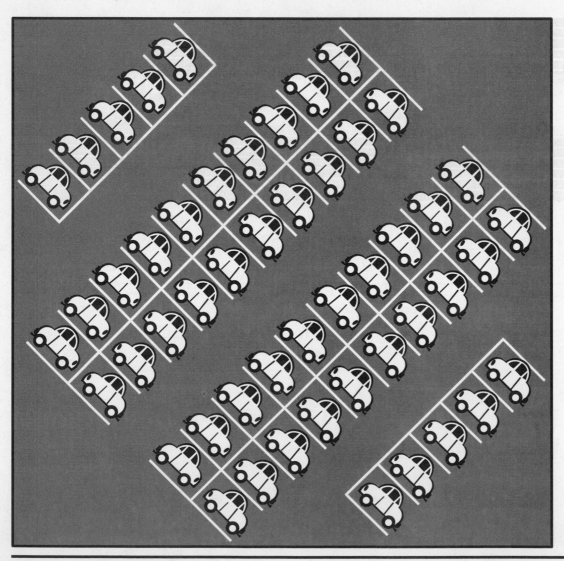 | green | .

Color 10 | red | .

Color 12 | blue | .

Color 9 | yellow | .

The rest of the are | purple | .

How many are | purple | ? ___

Add and Subtract in Circles

Start with the top number.

Look at the sign.

Add or subtract.

Write each missing number.

1.
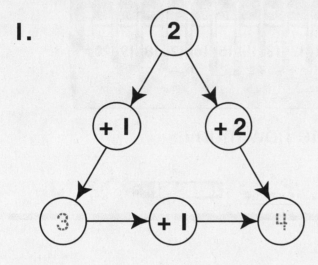

2.
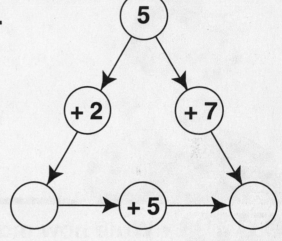

3.
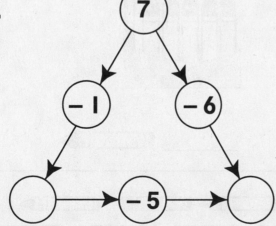

4.
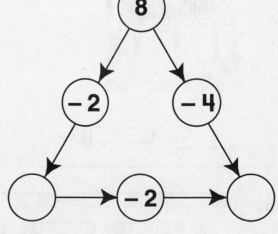

Name_____

Numbers to 20

Skill Builder **CHAPTER 6**

Learn

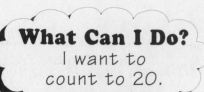

What Can I Do?
I want to count to 20.

Count one number for each.

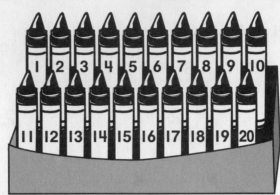

Write how many.

 20

Try It • Write how many.

1.

12

2.

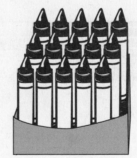

_____

3.

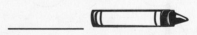

_____

© McGraw-Hill School Division

Power Practice • Write how many.

4.

_____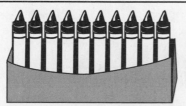

5.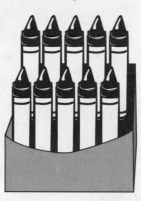

_____

6.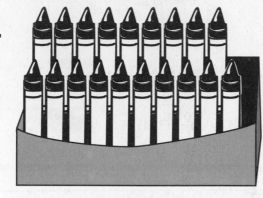

_____

7.

_____

8.

_____

9.

_____

10.

_____

More or Fewer

Learn

What Can I Do?
I want to find the group with more. I want to find the group with fewer.

Count how many in each.

7
6
5
4
3
2
1

5
4
3
2
1

Fewer means not as many.

7 is **more than** 5 .

5 is **fewer than** 7 .

Try It • **Circle the group that has more.**

I.

2.

Circle the group that has fewer.

3.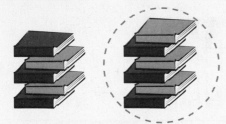

4.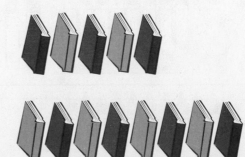

Name_____

5.

6.

7.

8.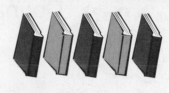

Circle the group that has fewer.

9.

10.

11.

12.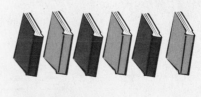

Name_____

Add Sums to 12

Skill Builder

CHAPTER **6**

Learn

_____ + _____ = _____

What Can I Do? I want to add.

Count how many in each.

$\underline{5}$ + $\underline{5}$ = _____

Add doubles.

$\underline{5}$ + $\underline{5}$ = $\underline{10}$

Try It Add. Write each sum.

1.

6 + 4 = $\underline{10}$

2. $\begin{array}{r} 6 \\ +6 \\ \hline \end{array}$

3. $8 + 3 =$ _____

4. $\begin{array}{r} 9 \\ +1 \\ \hline \end{array}$

© McGraw-Hill School Division

Name_____

Power Practice • Add. Write each sum.

5.  6.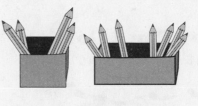

$7 + 5 = $ _____ $4 + 7 = $ _____

7. 8

$+2$

8. 6

$+3$

9. $8 + 4 = $ _____   10. $6 + 5 = $ _____

11. $7 + 1 = $ _____   12. $3 + 3 = $ _____

13. $7 + 4 = $ _____   14. $9 + 3 = $ _____

15. 8   16. 4   17. 5   18. 7

$+1$ $+4$ $+4$ $+3$

Subtract from 8

Learn

What Can I Do?
I want to subtract.

$8 - 2 =$ ____

Count back to subtract.

8 7 6

$8 - 2 =$ **6** ____

Try It • Subtract. Write each difference.

1.

$6 - 2 =$ ____

2.

$8 - 1 =$ ____

3. $\begin{array}{r} 8 \\ -3 \\ \hline \end{array}$

4. $\begin{array}{r} 5 \\ -4 \\ \hline \end{array}$

5. $6 - 3 =$ ____

6. $7 - 2 =$ ____

Power Practice • Subtract. Write each difference.

7. 

7 − 4 = _____

8.

5 − 3 = _____

9. 6
   −5

10. 4
   −2

11. 8 − 4 = _____

12. 7 − 1 = _____

13. 6 − 4 = _____

14. 8 − 6 = _____

15. 5 − 2 = _____

16. 4 − 1 = _____

17. 8
   −7

18. 6
   −1

19. 8
   −5

20. 7
   −3

Classroom Count

Count how many there are in your classroom.
Write how many.

1.

___

boys

2.

___

girls

3.

___

windows

4.

___

doors

5.

___

tables

6.

___

chairs

7.

___

bulletin boards

8.

___

plants

Name _____

A Difference Maze

Subtract. Write each difference.
Find each difference of 2.
Follow that path through the maze.

START

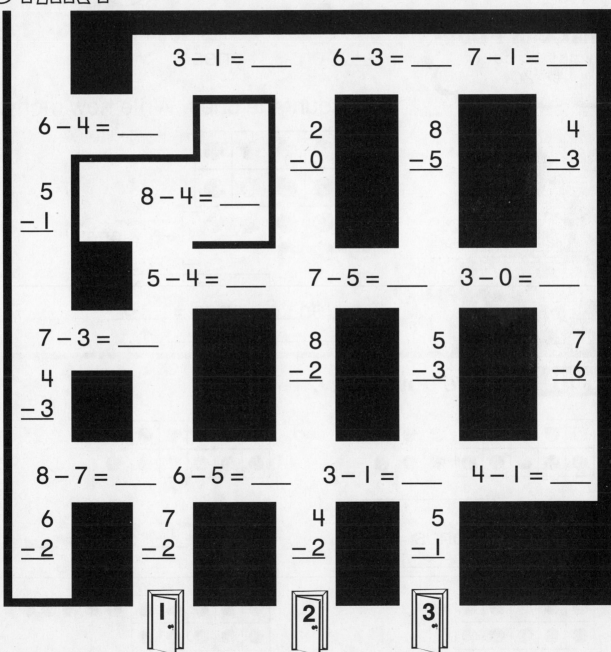

$3 - 1 =$ ___ $6 - 3 =$ ___ $7 - 1 =$ ___

$6 - 4 =$ ___

$\begin{array}{r} 2 \\ -0 \\ \hline \end{array}$ $\begin{array}{r} 8 \\ -5 \\ \hline \end{array}$ $\begin{array}{r} 4 \\ -3 \\ \hline \end{array}$

$\begin{array}{r} 5 \\ -1 \\ \hline \end{array}$

$8 - 4 =$ ___

$5 - 4 =$ ___ $7 - 5 =$ ___ $3 - 0 =$ ___

$7 - 3 =$ ___

$\begin{array}{r} 8 \\ -2 \\ \hline \end{array}$ $\begin{array}{r} 5 \\ -3 \\ \hline \end{array}$ $\begin{array}{r} 7 \\ -6 \\ \hline \end{array}$

$\begin{array}{r} 4 \\ -3 \\ \hline \end{array}$

$8 - 7 =$ ___ $6 - 5 =$ ___ $3 - 1 =$ ___ $4 - 1 =$ ___

$\begin{array}{r} 6 \\ -2 \\ \hline \end{array}$ $\begin{array}{r} 7 \\ -2 \\ \hline \end{array}$ $\begin{array}{r} 4 \\ -2 \\ \hline \end{array}$ $\begin{array}{r} 5 \\ -1 \\ \hline \end{array}$

1   2   3

Which door did you come out? ____

Count to 20

Learn

Count the tens first.

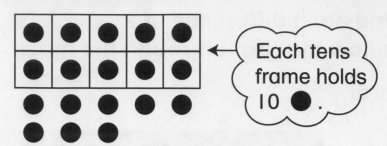

Each tens frame holds 10 ● .

___ ten ___ ones

What Can I Do?
I want to count to 20.

Now count the ones. Write how many.

8 ones

_1_ ten _8_ ones = _18_

Try It • Write how many.

1.

___ ten _6_ ones = _16_

2.

___ ten ___ ones = _____

3.

___ ten ___ ones = _____

4.

___ ten ___ ones = _____

Name_____

5.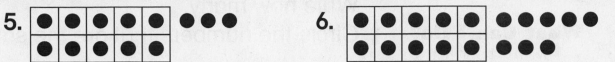

___ ten ___ ones = _____

6. ___ ten ___ ones = _____

7.

___ ten ___ ones = _____

8. ___ ten ___ ones = _____

9.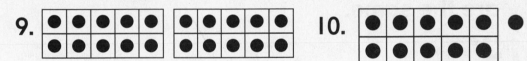

___ tens ___ ones = _____

10. ___ ten ___ one = _____

11.

___ ten ___ ones = _____

12. ___ ten ___ ones = _____

Same Number

Learn

What Can I Do?
I want to find numbers that are the same.

Write how many.
Circle the numbers that are the same.

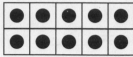

Try It • Write how many. Circle the numbers that are the same.

1.

15   10   15

Power Practice • Write how many. Circle the numbers that are the same.

2.

_____   _____   _____

3.

_____   _____   _____

More or Fewer

Learn

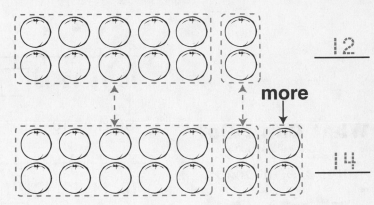

What Can I Do?
I want to find the group that has more.

Match. Write how many.

___12

more

___14

Circle the number that is more.

___12 ○   (___14) ○

Try It • Write how many. Circle the number that is more.

1. (___13)

   ___12

2. ___

   ___

Power Practice • Write how many. Circle the number that is more.

3.
   ___

   ___

4.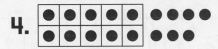
   ___

   ___

Order Numbers to 20

Learn

Count on to find the missing number.

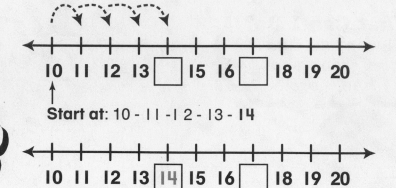

What Can I Do?
I want to write numbers in order.

Count on to find the missing number.

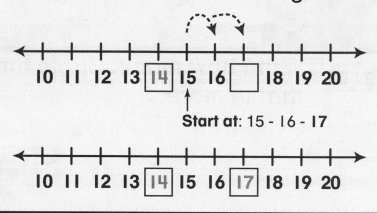

Try It • Write each missing number.

1.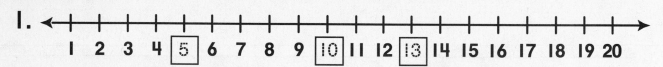

Power Practice • Write each missing number.

2.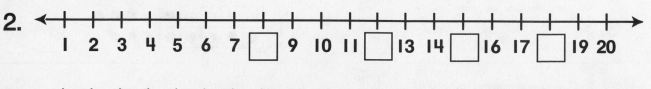

3.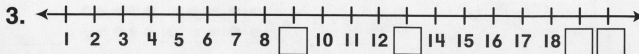

© McGraw-Hill School Division

Patterns

Learn

What Can I Do?
I want to find the next number in a pattern.

2 4 6 8 2 4 6 8 2 4 6 8 2 ___

Look for chunks.

2 4 6 8 2 4 6 8 2 4 6 8 2 ___

Look for a pattern.

2 4 6 8 2 4 6 8 2 4 6 8 2 ___

2 4 6 8 repeats.

Write the number that could come next.

2 4 6 8 2 4 6 8 2 4 6 8 2 _4_

Try It • **Write what the next number in the pattern could be.**

1. 3 1 3 2 3 1 3 2 3 1 3 2 3 1 3 _2_

Power Practice • **Write what the next number in the pattern could be.**

2. 4 5 4 5 4 5 4 5 4 ___

3. 5 6 7 5 6 7 5 6 7 5 6 ___

4. 11 12 11 12 11 12 11 12 11 12 11 ___

Compare Numbers to 20

Learn

Match to find the group with more.

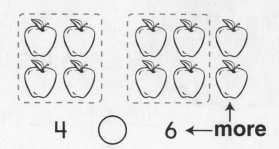

4 ◯ 6 ←**more**

Write > or < to show the group
with more or less.

6 is greater than 4.

    6 > 4

4 is less than 6.

So, 4 is ◯ 6.

What Can I Do?
I want to find the
group that has
more or less.

Try It • Write > or < .

1.

    6   ◯   5

2.

    15   ◯   12

3.

    16   ◯   18

4.

    12   ◯   14

Name________________________________

Power Practice • **Write > or < .**

5.

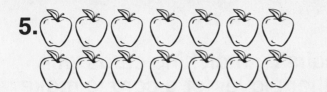

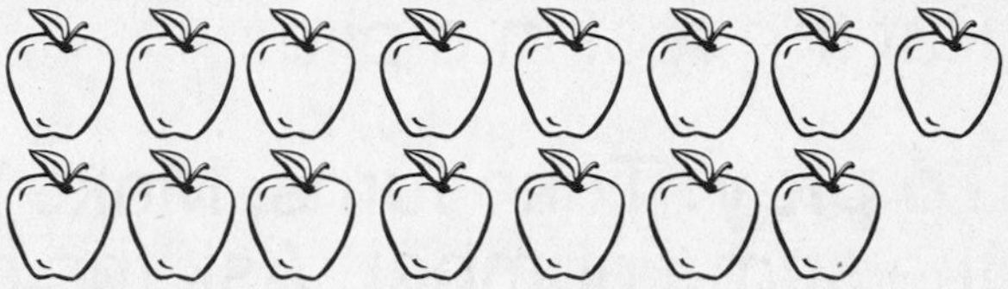

14 ◯ 15

6.

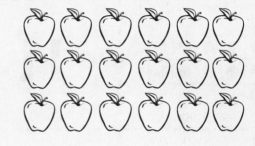

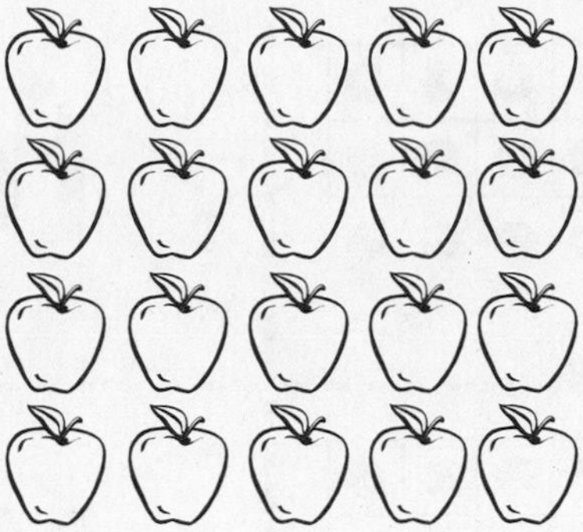

20 ◯ 18

7.

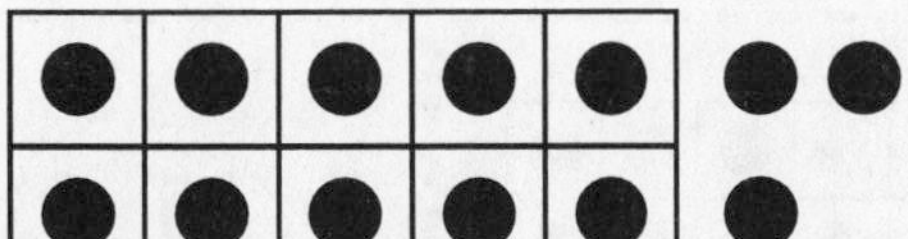

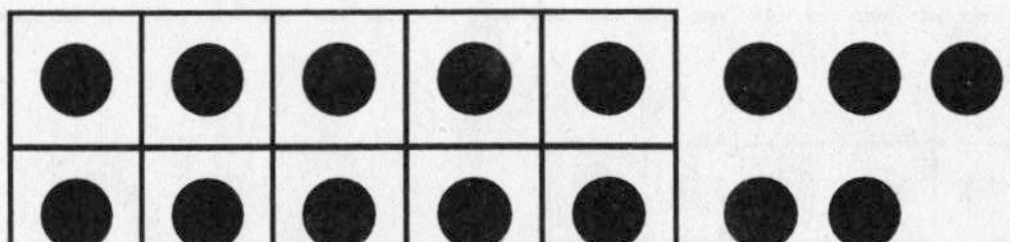

13 ◯ 15

8. 16 ◯ 12 **9.** 12 ◯ 13 **10.** 20 ◯ 19

11. 17 ◯ 15 **12.** 16 ◯ 17 **13.** 17 ◯ 18

Name_____

Go Fish for Numbers

Cut out the cards. Give 3 cards to each player.
Put the rest in a pile.

To play: Take turns. Make pairs by matching cards with the same number. Ask the other player for a card to make a match. If the other player doesn't have the card you asked for, go fish.

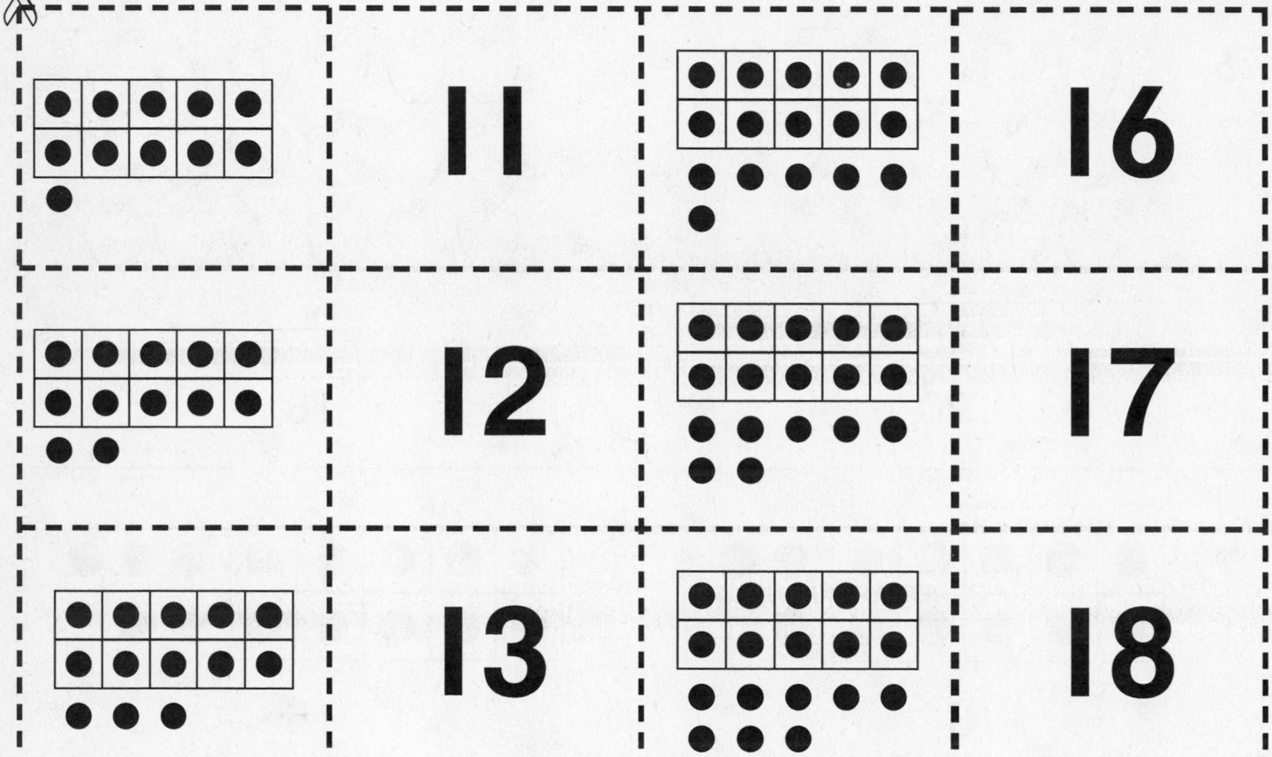

	11		16
	12		17
	13		18
	14		19
	15		20

Secret Number Code

Write the numbers in each box in order.
Write the numbers from least to greatest.

1.

8	10
11	9

_8_ _9_ (10) _11_

2.

16	17
15	14

___ ___ ( ) ___

3.

13	11
10	12

___ ___ ( ) ___

4.

20	17
19	18

___ ___ ( ) ___

5.

15	10
5	20

___ ___ ( ) ___

6.

6	2
8	4

___ ___ ( ) ___

3 = S
4 = R
6 = Y
9 = A
10 = T
11 = P
12 = E
14 = O
15 = T
16 = W
19 = N
20 = F

Match the numbers in the circles to the letters in the box.
Write the letters on the lines below. Find the secret number.

___ ___ ___ ___ ___ ___
1. 2. 3. 4. 5. 6.

Skip Count by 5s

Learn

What Can I Do?
I want to skip count by fives.

Skip count by fives.
Write each missing number.

5 10 ____ 20 25 ____

Look for a pattern.

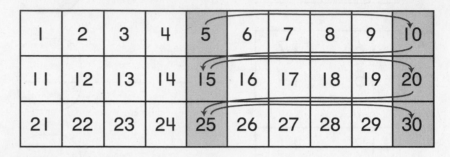

1	2	3	4	5	6	7	8	9	10
11	12	13	14	15	16	17	18	19	20
21	22	23	24	25	26	27	28	29	30

5 10 _15_ 20 25 _30_

Try It • Skip count by fives.
Write each missing number.

1. 5 10 15 _20_ 25 30 _35_ 40

2. 45 50 ____ 60 65 70 ____ ____

Power Practice • Skip count by fives.
Write each missing number.

3. 5 10 15 20 ____ 30 35 ____ ____

4. 50 55 60 ____ 70 75 80 ____ ____

Skip Count by 10s

Learn

What Can I Do?
I want to skip count by tens.

Skip count by tens. Write each missing number.

10 20 30 ____ ____

Look for a pattern.

1	2	3	4	5	6	7	8	9	10
11	12	13	14	15	16	17	18	19	20
21	22	23	24	25	26	27	28	29	30
31	32	33	34	35	36	37	38	39	40
41	42	43	44	45	46	47	48	49	50

10 20 30 _40_ _50_

Try It • Skip count by tens. Write each missing number.

1. 10 20 _30_ 40 _50_

2. 50 60 ____ ____ 90

Power Practice • Skip count by tens. Write each missing number.

3. 10 ____ 30 40 50 ____

4. 10 20 ____ ____ ____ 70 ____ ____ ____

Number Patterns: I More

Learn

What Can I Do?
I want to find 1 more than a number.

Find I more than 20.

First, find 20.

1	2	3	4	5	6	7	8	9	10
11	12	13	14	15	16	17	18	19	20
21	22	23	24	25	26	27	28	29	30
31	32	33	34	35	36	37	38	39	40
41	42	43	44	45	46	47	48	49	50

Count on I to find I more.

I more than 20 is __21__ .

Try It • Write each number.

I. I more than 30 __31__

2. I more than 35 ____

Power Practice • Write each number.

3. I more than 25 ____

4. I more than 50 ____

5. I more than 45 ____

6. I more than 80 ____

7. I more than 75 ____

8. I more than 40 ____

Name_____

Number Patterns: 10 More

Learn

What Can I Do?
I want to find 10 more than a number.

Find 10 more than 35.

First, find 35.

1	2	3	4	5	6	7	8	9	10
11	12	13	14	15	16	17	18	19	20
21	22	23	24	25	26	27	28	29	30
31	32	33	34	35	36	37	38	39	40
41	42	43	44	45	46	47	48	49	50

10 more

Count on by tens to find 10 more.

10 more than 35 is __45__ .

Try It • Write each number.

1. 10 more than 5 __15__   **2.** 10 more than 15 ____

Power Practice • Write each number.

3. 10 more than 25 ____   **4.** 10 more than 30 ____

5. 10 more than 45 ____   **6.** 10 more than 50 ____

7. 10 more than 75 ____   **8.** 10 more than 90 ____

Compare Numbers to 100

Learn

Write how many.

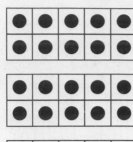 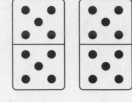

 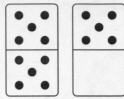

_32_ ◯ _35_

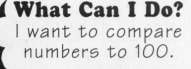

What Can I Do?
I want to compare numbers to 100.

Compare the tens.

3 tens 2 ones   3 tens 5 ones

3 tens = 3 tens

Compare the ones.

3 tens 2 ones   3 tens 5 ones

2 ones < 5 ones

So, 32 ⊘ 35.

Try It • Write how many.
Write >, <, or = .

1.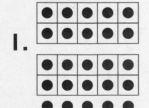

_25_ ◯ _25_

2.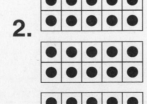

___ ◯ ___

Power Practice • Write how many.
Write >, <, or = .

3.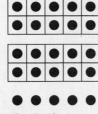

____ ◯ ____

4.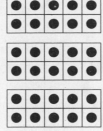

____ ◯ ____

5.

____ ◯ ____

6.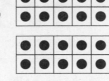

____ ◯ ____

Write >, <, or = .

7. 8 ◯ 7   **8.** 10 ◯ 10   **9.** 9 ◯ 10

10. 10 ◯ 11   **11.** 15 ◯ 13   **12.** 18 ◯ 17

13. 21 ◯ 20   **14.** 25 ◯ 28   **15.** 26 ◯ 24

16. 30 ◯ 29   **17.** 36 ◯ 35   **18.** 40 ◯ 40

Add Sums to 12

Learn

What Can I Do?
I want to add.

4 + 8 = _____

Put the groups together.
Count how many.

Write how many in all.

4 + 8 = _12_

Try It • Add. Write each sum.

1.

5 + 4 = _9_

2.

6 + 6 = _____

3. 7 + 3 = _____

4. 9 + 2 = _____

5. 4
   +4
   ___

6. 6
   +3
   ___

Name_____

Power Practice · Add. Write each sum.

7.

$7 + 4 =$ ___

8.

$5 + 3 =$ ___

9.

$8 + 2 =$ ___

10.

$6 + 4 =$ ___

11. $9 + 3 =$ ___   **12.** $3 + 6 =$ ___

13. $6 + 5 =$ ___   **14.** $4 + 3 =$ ___

15. $8 + 3 =$ ___   **16.** $7 + 5 =$ ___

17. $\begin{array}{r} 8 \\ +4 \\ \hline \end{array}$ **18.** $\begin{array}{r} 9 \\ +1 \\ \hline \end{array}$ **19.** $\begin{array}{r} 3 \\ +3 \\ \hline \end{array}$ **20.** $\begin{array}{r} 4 \\ +2 \\ \hline \end{array}$

Name_____

Subtract from 12

Learn

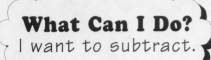

What Can I Do?
I want to subtract.

12 − 3 = _____

Cross out to subtract.

Write how many are left.

12 − 3 = __9__

Try It • **Subtract. Write the difference.**

1.

10 − 4 = __6__

2.

11 − 8 = _____

3. 12 − 5 = _____

4. 7 − 6 = _____

5.   9
  − 2

6. 11
  − 4

Power Practice • Subtract. Write the difference.

7.

$12 - 4 = $ ___

8.

$10 - 5 = $ ___

9.

$8 - 6 = $ ___

10.

$11 - 2 = $ ___

11. $10 - 3 = $ ___

12. $12 - 6 = $ ___

13. $12 - 9 = $ ___

14. $11 - 7 = $ ___

15. $8 - 1 = $ ___

16. $11 - 5 = $ ___

17. $\begin{array}{r} 11 \\ -3 \\ \hline \end{array}$

18. $\begin{array}{r} 10 \\ -8 \\ \hline \end{array}$

19. $\begin{array}{r} 7 \\ -7 \\ \hline \end{array}$

20. $\begin{array}{r} 12 \\ -8 \\ \hline \end{array}$

Name_____

Toy Store Game

Play with a partner.

Cut out the cards.

Put them face down in a pile.

Player 1 uses 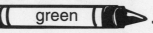 green.

Player 2 uses 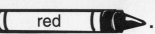 red.

To Play:
Take turns. Take 1 card from the pile. Find something in the store to buy for that amount. Color it.

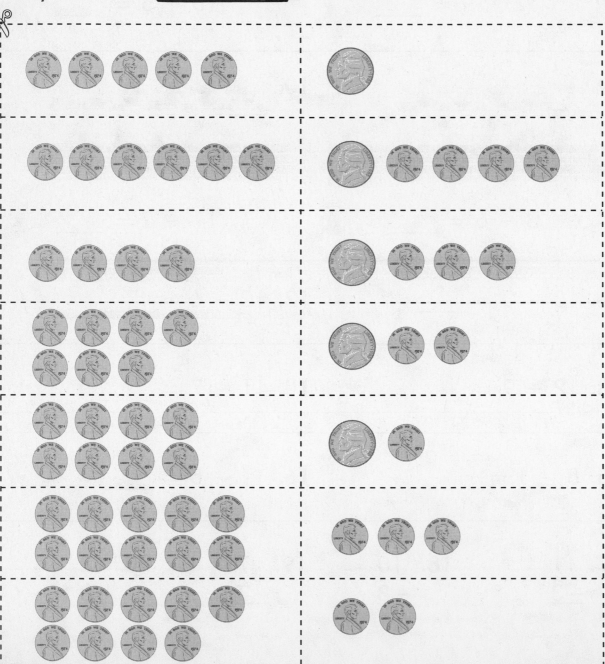

Lee's Toys

Addition Search

Circle the addition facts in the puzzle.

Look → and ↓.

6	3	9	4	3	2	8	7	2	1	3	4	5	3	8
5	4	9	6	4	4	9	1	2	1	8	9	6	1	2
2	5	7	8	7	3	1	8	5	3	4	2	6	7	7
1	2	3	9	4	4	8	5	7	1	1	2	5	8	9
8	1	9	3	6	5	9	2	6	8	9	6	2	8	7
6	3	4	6	8	4	1	5	5	5	2	7	8	4	3
3	2	7	5	1	4	5	1	3	4	3	4	3	6	9
7	5	5	1	7	9	4	6	1	7	1	5	6	5	5
3	3	8	6	9	2	6	3	5	7	9	4	5	9	3
1	9	2	9	1	1	2	5	6	8	2	8	5	3	9
4	5	2	5	3	7	3	8	4	3	7	1	2	3	5
3	5	2	6	5	4	5	2	4	6	3	6	4	7	8
2	8	4	7	2	9	7	2	1	4	3	7	3	3	6

On Sale at the Toy Store

Each  has  for toys.

Cut out a toy for each to buy.

Paste it in the box.

Then write the subtraction problem to show

how much each 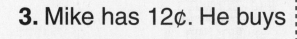 has left.

5¢

7¢

1. Tom has 10¢. He buys [ ] .

10¢ − ____ = ____

4¢

2. Jan has 8¢. She buys [ ] .

8¢ − ____ = ____

3¢

3. Mike has 12¢. He buys [ ] .

12¢ − ____ = ____

6¢

4. Sue has 11¢. She buys [ ] .

11¢ − ____ = ____

8¢

5. Kim has 9¢. She buys [ ] .

9¢ − ____ = ____

Count to 20

Learn

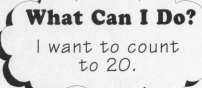

What Can I Do?

I want to count to 20.

Count 1 number for each.

1	2	3	4	5
6	7	8	9	10
11	12	13	14	15
16	17	18	19	20

Write how many.

_20_

Try It • Write how many.

1.

_12_

2.

_____

Power Practice • Write how many.

3.

_____

4.

_____

5.

_____

Patterns

Learn

What Can I Do?
I want to find the next number in a pattern.

2 2 4 2 2 4 2 2 4 2 2 ___

Look for chunks.

|2 2 4||2 2 4||2 2 4||2 2 ___|

Find the pattern.

|2 2 4||2 2 4||2 2 4||2 2 ___|

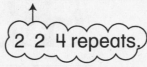

2 2 4 repeats.

Write the number that could come next in the pattern.

|2 2 4||2 2 4||2 2 4||2 2 _4_|

Try It • Write the number that could come next in the pattern.

1. |3 4 7||3 4 7||3 4 7||3 4 _7_|

2. 3 3 6 3 3 6 3 3 6 3 3 ___

Power Practice • Write the number that could come next in the pattern.

3. 2 3 5 2 3 5 2 3 5 2 3 ___

4. 4 4 8 4 4 8 4 4 8 4 4 ___

5. 4 5 9 4 5 9 4 5 9 4 5 ___

Name_____

Add Sums to 12

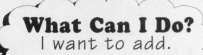 **Learn**

What Can I Do?
I want to add.

$$6 \quad + \quad 4 \quad = \quad \_\_\_$$

Put the groups together. Count how many.

Write how many in all.

$$6 \quad + \quad 4 \quad = \quad \underline{10}$$ 🍅

Try It • Add. Write each sum.

1.

$$5 + 7 = \underline{12}$$

2. $$\begin{array}{r} 8 \\ +4 \\ \hline \end{array}$$ 🍅🍅🍅🍅🍅🍅🍅🍅
🍅🍅🍅🍅

Power Practice • Add. Write each sum.

3.

$$7 + 4 = \_\_\_$$

4. $$\begin{array}{r} 3 \\ +5 \\ \hline \end{array}$$ 🍅🍅🍅
🍅🍅🍅🍅🍅

---

5. $$\begin{array}{r} 3 \\ +6 \\ \hline \end{array}$$

6. $$\begin{array}{r} 9 \\ +3 \\ \hline \end{array}$$

7. $$\begin{array}{r} 5 \\ +6 \\ \hline \end{array}$$

8. $$\begin{array}{r} 8 \\ +2 \\ \hline \end{array}$$

Add Sums to 12: Counting On

Learn

What Can I Do?
I want to count on to add.

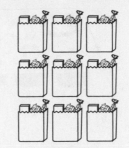

$$9 \quad + \quad 2 \quad = \quad \underline{}$$

Start at 9. Count on 2.

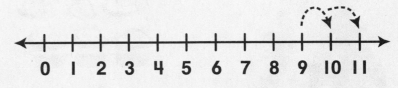

So, $9 + 2 = \underline{11}$

Try It • Count on to add. Write each sum.

1.

$$6 + 1 = \underline{7}$$

2. $\begin{array}{r} 7 \\ +3 \\ \hline \end{array}$

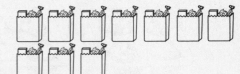

Power Practice • Count on to add. Write each sum.

3. $8 + 2 = \underline{}$ **4.** $6 + 2 = \underline{}$

---

5. $\begin{array}{r} 5 \\ +3 \\ \hline \end{array}$ **6.** $\begin{array}{r} 4 \\ +2 \\ \hline \end{array}$ **7.** $\begin{array}{r} 8 \\ +3 \\ \hline \end{array}$ **8.** $\begin{array}{r} 7 \\ +2 \\ \hline \end{array}$

Add Sums to 12: Doubles

Learn

What Can I Do?
I want to add doubles.

6 + 6 = ___

The addends are the same.
Add the doubles.

6 + 6 = _12_

Try It • Add. Write each sum.

1.

4 + 4 = _8_

2. 5
   +5

Power Practice • Add. Write each sum.

3. 1 + 1 = ___

4. 5 + 5 = ___

5. 3
   +3

6. 6
   +6

7. 2
   +2

8. 4
   +4

Add Sums to 12: Doubles + 1

Learn

What Can I Do?
I want to add doubles plus 1.

6   +   5 = ____ 🍍

Find a double that is close to 6 + 5.

5 + 5 = 10

6 is 1 more than 5.
Count on 1 more
from the sum:
10, 11

6   +   5 = __11__ 🍍

Try It • Add. Write each sum.

1.

   2 + 3 = __5__ 🍍

2. 4
   +5

Power Practice • Add. Write each sum.

3. 3 + 4 = ____   **4.** 1 + 2 = ____

5. 5   **6.** 3   **7.** 2   **8.** 4
    +6   +2   +1   +3

Subtract from 12

Learn

What Can I Do?
I want to
subtract.

$12 - 3 =$ _____

Cross out to subtract.
Write how many are left.

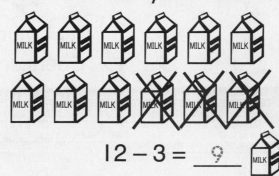

$12 - 3 =$ _9_

Try It • Subtract. Write the difference.

1.

$10 - 6 =$ _____

2. 8
  $- 5$

3. $11 - 7 =$ _____

4. $10 - 8 =$ _____

5. 7
  $- 5$

6. 5
  $- 4$

7. 12
  $- 7$

8. 10
  $- 9$

Name_____

Power Practice • Subtract. Write the difference.

9.
8 − 6 = _____

10.
10 − 4 = _____

11. 12
   − 5

12. 11
    − 5

13. 11 − 9 = _____

14. 10 − 7 = _____

15. 8 − 7 = _____

16. 12 − 8 = _____

17. 7 − 4 = _____

18. 11 − 6 = _____

19. 11
    − 4

20. 7
    − 6

21. 12
    − 9

22. 6
    − 4

23. 12
    − 4

24. 6
    − 5

25. 5
    − 4

26. 11
    − 8

Count Back to Subtract

Learn

What Can I Do?
I want to count back to subtract.

10 − 3 = _____

Start at 10. Count back 3.

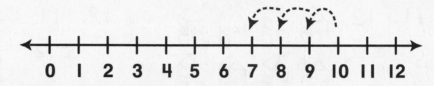

0 1 2 3 4 5 6 7 8 9 10 11 12

So, 10 − 3 = __7__

Try It · Count back to subtract. Write each difference.

1.

8 − 2 = __6__

2. 11
   − 3

Power Practice · Count back to subtract. Write each difference.

3. 9 − 3 = _____   **4.** 7 − 2 = _____

---

5. 9   **6.** 11   **7.** 6   **8.** 10
      − 1   − 2   − 1   − 2

Subtract from 12: Doubles

Learn

What Can I Do?
I want to subtract.

$8 - 4 = $ _____

Think about addition doubles.

$8 - 4 = $ _____

$4 + 4 = 8$

Subtract. Write the difference.

$8 - 4 = $ __4__

Try It • Subtract. Write each difference.

1.
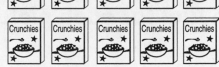

$10 - 5 = $ _____

2. $\begin{array}{r} 6 \\ -3 \\ \hline \end{array}$

Power Practice • Subtract. Write each difference.

3. $4 - 2 = $ _____

4. $12 - 6 = $ _____

5. $\begin{array}{r} 2 \\ -1 \\ \hline \end{array}$

6. $\begin{array}{r} 8 \\ -4 \\ \hline \end{array}$

7. $\begin{array}{r} 10 \\ -5 \\ \hline \end{array}$

8. $\begin{array}{r} 12 \\ -6 \\ \hline \end{array}$

Related Addition Facts

Learn

What Can I Do?
I want to
use related
facts to add.

1 + 3 = ____

Change the order.
Write the new fact.

3 + 1 = ____

Add.

1 + 3 = 4

3 + 1 = 4

Try It • Complete the addition fact for each picture.

1.

2 + 4 = 6

4 + 2 = 6

2.

5 + 2 = ___

2 + 5 = ___

3.

$$\begin{array}{r} 2 \\ +6 \\ \hline \end{array}$$ $$\begin{array}{r} 6 \\ +2 \\ \hline \end{array}$$

Name_____

Power Practice • Complete the addition fact for each picture.

4.

4 + 6 = ____

6 + 4 = ____

5.

7 + 1 = ____

1 + 7 = ____

6.

4	7
+7	+4

7.

2	8
+8	+2

8. 9 + 3 = ____

3 + 9 = ____

9. 5 + 4 = ____

4 + 5 = ____

10. 3 + 5 = ____

5 + 3 = ____

11. 7 + 2 = ____

2 + 7 = ____

12.

8	1
+1	+8

13.

9	2
+2	+9

14.

4	8
+8	+4

Related Subtraction Facts

Learn

What Can I Do?
I want to use related facts to subtract.

Subtract

$10 - 6 = $ _____

$10 - 4 = $ _____

Look for related facts.

$10 - 6 = $ _____

$10 - 4 = $ _____

Try It • Complete two subtraction facts for each picture.

1.

$7 - 3 = $ _4_

$7 - 4 = $ _3_

2.

$11 - 5 = $ _____

$11 - 6 = $ _____

3.

$$
\begin{array}{c} 11 \\ -4 \\ \hline \end{array}
\qquad
\begin{array}{c} 11 \\ -7 \\ \hline \end{array}
$$

4.

$$
\begin{array}{c} 10 \\ -8 \\ \hline \end{array}
\qquad
\begin{array}{c} 10 \\ -2 \\ \hline \end{array}
$$

Name_____

Power Practice • **Complete two subtraction facts for each picture.**

5.

$9 - 3 =$ _____

$9 - 6 =$ _____

6.

$6 - 4 =$ _____

$6 - 2 =$ _____

7.

12	12
-9	-3

8.

8	8
-3	-5

9. $5 - 3 =$ _____

$5 - 2 =$ _____

10. $10 - 9 =$ _____

$10 - 1 =$ _____

11. $12 - 5 =$ _____

$12 - 7 =$ _____

12. $9 - 5 =$ _____

$9 - 4 =$ _____

13.

11	11
-8	-3

14.

7	7
-2	-5

15.

12	12
-4	-8

Missing Addends

Learn

What Can I Do?
I want to find the missing addend in the addition.

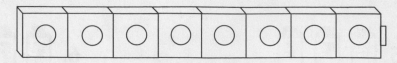

$\boxed{5} + 3 = 8$

Subtract to find the missing addend.

$\boxed{} + 3 = 8$

$8 - 3 = \boxed{5}$

So, $\boxed{5} + 3 = 8$

Try It • Write each missing number.

1.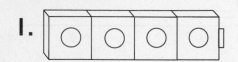

$\boxed{3} + 1 = 4$

$4 - 1 = \boxed{3}$

2.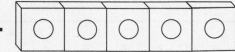

$\boxed{} + 3 = 5$

$5 - 3 = \boxed{}$

3.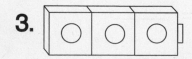

$\begin{array}{r} 2 \\ + \boxed{} \\ \hline 3 \end{array}$
$\qquad$
$\begin{array}{r} 3 \\ - 2 \\ \hline \boxed{} \end{array}$

4.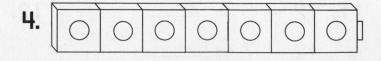

$\begin{array}{r} 4 \\ + \boxed{} \\ \hline 7 \end{array}$
$\qquad$
$\begin{array}{r} 7 \\ - 4 \\ \hline \boxed{} \end{array}$

Power Practice • **Write each missing number.**

5. ⬜ + 1 = 5

5 − 1 = ⬜

6. ⬜ + 2 = 7

7 − 2 = ⬜

7.

  1   4
+⬜   −1
──   ──
  4   ⬜

8.

  2   6
+⬜   −2
──   ──
  6   ⬜

9. ⬜ + 2 = 8

8 − 2 = ⬜

10. ⬜ + 6 = 10

10 − 6 = ⬜

11. ⬜ + 5 = 11

11 − 5 = ⬜

12. ⬜ + 3 = 9

9 − 3 = ⬜

13.

  6   8
+⬜   −2
──   ──
  8

14.

  3   10
+⬜   −7
──   ──
 10

15.

  4   9
+⬜   −4
──   ──
  9

Go Shopping!

Cut out the cards.
Mix them up.
Put them face down in a pile.
Play with a partner.

To play:
Take turns.
Turn over 1 card. Add.
If you are correct, move the number of spaces shown.

4 + 8	Move 3	3 + 7	Move 2	1 + 8	Move 1
6 + 4	Move 3	3 + 9	Move 2	9 + 1	Move 1
8 + 3	Move 2	4 + 5	Move 3	7 + 3	Move 2
5 + 5	Move 2	7 + 2	Move 1	5 + 1	Move 1
2 + 2	Move 2	2 + 9	Move 1	9 + 3	Move 2
6 + 6	Move 2	8 + 2	Move 1	1 + 6	Move 1

Name______________________________

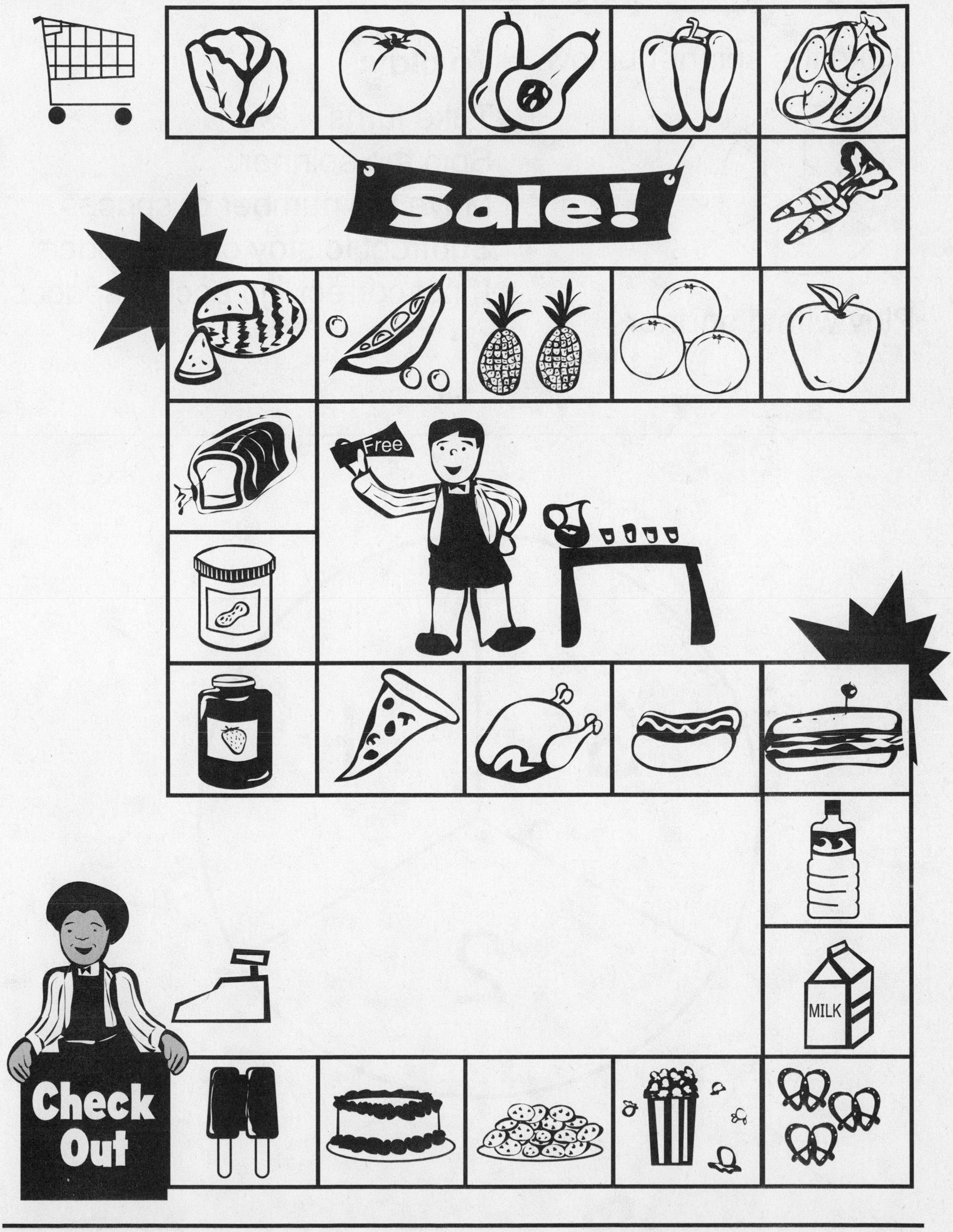

All Around the Mall

Use a ⌒▭ and a ▱▭ .

Make the spinner below.

Play with a partner.

To play:

Take turns.
Spin the spinner.
Move the number of spaces.
Subtract to stay on the space.
If not correct, go back 3 spaces.

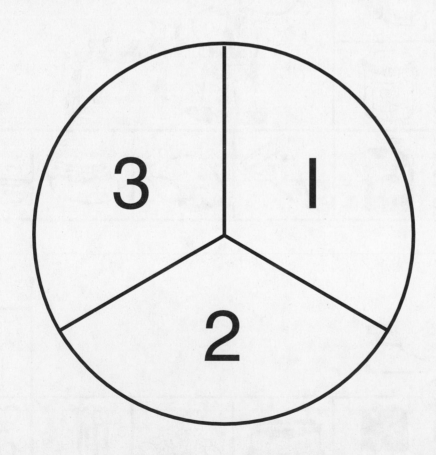

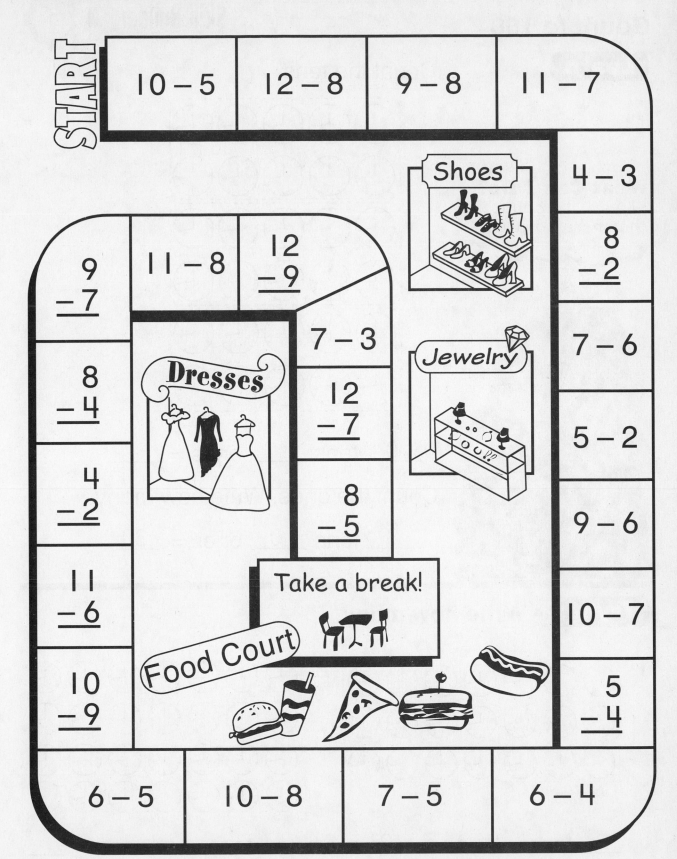

START

10 − 5 | 12 − 8 | 9 − 8 | 11 − 7

4 − 3

8
−2

7 − 6

5 − 2

9 − 6

10 − 7

5
−4

Shoes

Jewelry

9
−7

11 − 8

12
−9

7 − 3

12
−7

8
−5

Dresses

Take a break!

Food Court

8
−4

4
−2

11
−6

10
−9

6 − 5 | 10 − 8 | 7 − 5 | 6 − 4

Count to 100

Learn

Count the tens.

____3____ tens _____ ones = _____

Count the ones. Write how many.

____3____ tens ____0____ ones = ____30____

What Can I Do?
I want to count numbers to 100.

Try It • **Write how many.**

1.

____2____ tens ____1____ one = ____21____

2.

_____ tens _____ ones = _____

© McGraw-Hill School Division

Power Practice • **Write how many.**

3. ⏰⏰⏰⏰⏰⏰⏰
⏰⏰⏰⏰⏰⏰
⏰⏰⏰⏰⏰⏰
⏰⏰⏰⏰⏰⏰
⏰⏰⏰

____ tens ____ one = ____

4. ⏰⏰⏰⏰⏰⏰⏰
⏰⏰⏰⏰⏰⏰
⏰⏰⏰⏰

____ ten ____ ones = ____

5. ⏰⏰⏰⏰⏰
⏰⏰⏰⏰⏰
⏰⏰

____ ten ____ ones = ____

6. ⏰⏰⏰⏰⏰⏰⏰
⏰⏰⏰⏰⏰⏰⏰

____ ten ____ ones = ____

7. ⏰⏰⏰⏰⏰⏰⏰
⏰⏰⏰⏰⏰⏰⏰
⏰⏰⏰⏰⏰⏰⏰
⏰⏰⏰⏰

____ tens ____ ones = ____

8. ⏰⏰⏰⏰⏰
⏰⏰⏰⏰⏰
⏰⏰⏰⏰⏰
⏰⏰⏰⏰⏰

____ tens ____ ones = ____

Same Number

Learn

What Can I Do?
I want to find the same numbers.

Write how many in each.

_10_   _9_   _10_

Circle the same number.

   9

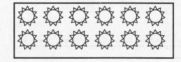

Try It • **Write how many. Circle the same numbers.**

1.

_12_   _8_   _12_

Power Practice • **Write how many.**
Circle the same numbers.

2.  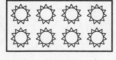   3.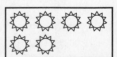

_____   _____

Before and After

Learn

What Can I Do?
I want to find who comes before and after.

Who is before Tom?

Look ← to find the one before.

Jean   **Tom**   Pat   Greg

Jean is before Tom.

Try It • Write who comes before or after.

Greg   Jean   Pat   Tom

1. After Pat _____   2. Before Jean _____

Power Practice • Write who comes before or after.

Jean   Pat   Greg   Tom

3. After Greg _____   4. Before Pat _____

Name_____

Ordinals

Learn

What Can I Do?
I want to
find who is
fourth.

Jill   Ann   Rob   Tim   Deb

Count to find the fourth one.

Jill   Ann   Rob   Tim   Deb
↑   ↑   ↑   ↑   ↑
first second third **fourth** fifth

Tim is fourth.

Try It • **Write the name of the person.**

Sam Jon Pam Dan Ann Mai Deb Rob Tim Jill

1. I am first. __Sam__

2. I am sixth. _____

3. I am fourth. _____

4. I am tenth. _____

5. I am second. _____

6. I am third. _____

Name_____

Power Practice • Write the name of the person.

Pam Rob Mai Sam Dan Deb Tim Ann Jill Jon

7. I am second.

_____

8. I am sixth.

_____

9. I am seventh.

_____

10. I am eighth.

_____

11. I am ninth.

_____

12. I am first.

_____

13. I am fifth.

_____

14. I am third.

_____

Name_____

Order Numbers to 100

Learn

1	2	3	4	5	6	7	8	9	10
11	12	13	14	15	16	17	18	19	20
21	22	23	24	25	26	27	28	29	30
31	32	33	34	35	36	37	38	39	40
41	42	43	44	45	46	47	48	49	50

What Can I Do?
I want to write the numbers that come just before and just after a number.

Count back to find the number just before 34.

33 34

33 is just before 34.

Count back to find the number just before 34.

33 34

35 is just after 34.

_____33_____ 34 _____35_____

Try It • Write the number that comes just before.

1. __20__ 21   **2.** _____ 36   **3.** _____ 50

Write the number that comes just after.

4. 15 _____   **5.** 30 _____   **6.** 44 _____

Write the number that comes between.

7. 36 _____ 38   **8.** 39 _____ 41

Name_____

9. _____ 28   **10.** _____ 40

1	2	3	4	5	6	7	8	9	10
11	12	13	14	15	16	17	18	19	20
21	22	23	24	25	26	27	28	29	30
31	32	33	34	35	36	37	38	39	40
41	42	43	44	45	46	47	48	49	50
51	52	53	54	55	56	57	58	59	60

11. _____ 14   **12.** _____ 23

13. _____ 31   **14.** _____ 13   **15.** _____ 26

Write the number that comes just after.

16. 54 _____   **17.** 40 _____   **18.** 10 _____

19. 22 _____   **20.** 46 _____   **21.** 59 _____

Write the number that comes between.

22. 50 _____ 52   **23.** 28 _____ 30

24. 42 _____ 44   **25.** 20 _____ 22

Estimate Time

Learn

What Can I Do?
I want to estimate how long it takes to do something.

I brush my hair.
About 1 **minute**.

I am sick.
About 1 **day**

I play a game.
About 1 **hour**

Try It . Circle the time it would take to do each activity.

1. I ride my bike.

(about 1 hour)

about 1 day

2. I write my name.

about 1 minute

about 1 hour

Name_____

Power Practice • Circle the time it would take to do each activity.

3. I read a book.

about I minute

about I hour

4. I put on my socks.

about I minute

about I hour

5. I go to Grandma's house.

about I minute

about I day

6. I wash my face.

about I minute

about I hour

7. I fill a glass.

about I minute

about I hour

8. I watch a TV show.

about I hour

about I day

Mystery Numbers

Read each clue.
Find each mystery number.

1. I am after 30.
   I am before 35.
   I am **not** between 32 and 34.
   If you add my numbers, the sum is 4.
   What number am I? _____

2. I am after 20.
   I am before 40.
   One of my numbers is zero.
   What number am I? _____

3. I am after 10.
   I am before 20.
   I am **not** after 13.
   I am **not** 11.
   What number am I? _____

4. I am between 20 and 30.
   If you add my numbers, the sum is 11.
   What number am I? _____

Name________________________________

Picturing Time

CHAPTER 10 CHALLENGE

Draw a picture of something you do for each time that is shown.
Write a sentence about each picture.

About 1 minute

____

____

About 1 hour

____

____

Count to 100

Learn

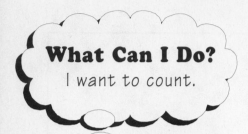

What Can I Do?
I want to count.

Count the tens.

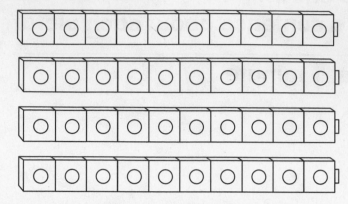

___4___ tens _____ ones = _____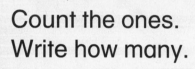

Count the ones.
Write how many.

___4___ tens ___0___ ones = ___40___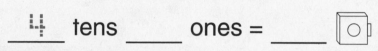

Try It • **Write how many.**

1.

___6___ tens ___0___ ones = ___60___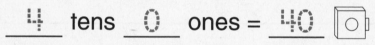

2.

_____ tens _____ ones = _____

Power Practice • **Write how many.**

3. ▭▭▭▭▭▭▭▭▭▭ ▭▭▭▭▭▭▭▭▭▭ ▭▭▭▭▭▭▭▭▭▭

▭▭▭▭▭▭▭▭▭▭ ▭▭▭▭▭▭▭▭▭▭

____ tens ____ ones = ____ ▭

4. ▭▭▭▭▭▭▭▭▭▭ ▭▭▭▭▭▭▭▭▭▭ ▭▭▭▭▭▭▭▭▭▭

▭▭▭▭▭▭▭▭▭▭ ▭▭▭▭▭▭▭▭▭▭ ▭▭▭▭▭▭▭▭▭▭

▭▭▭▭▭▭▭▭▭▭

____ tens ____ ones = ____ ▭

5. ▭▭▭▭▭▭▭▭▭▭ ▭▭▭▭▭▭▭▭▭▭ ▭▭▭▭▭▭▭▭▭▭

▭▭▭▭▭▭▭▭▭▭ ▭▭▭▭▭▭▭▭▭▭ ▭▭▭▭▭▭▭▭▭▭

▭▭▭▭▭▭▭▭▭▭ ▭▭▭▭▭▭▭▭▭▭ ▭▭▭▭▭▭▭▭▭▭

____ tens ____ ones = ____ ▭

Longer or Shorter

Learn

Line up the objects on one side.

What Can I Do?
I want to find the object that is longer.

Circle the one that is longer.

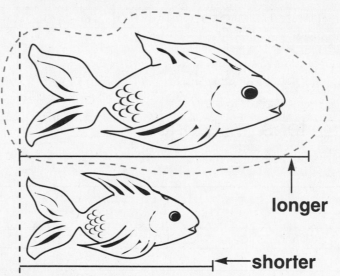

longer

shorter

Try It • Circle the one that is longer.

1.

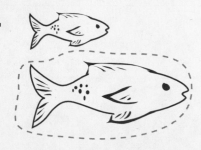

2.

Power Practice • Circle the one that is longer.

3.
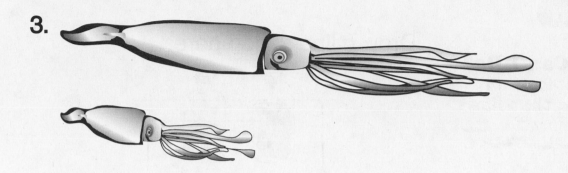

4.
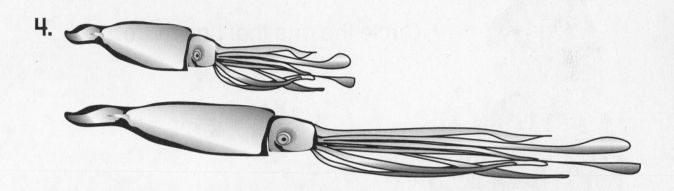

Circle the one that is shorter.

5.
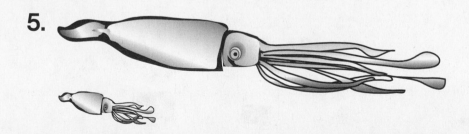

6. 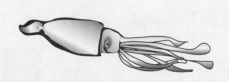   7.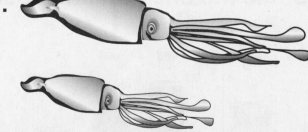

More Than, Less Than, About the Same As

Learn

What Can I Do?
I want to find the one that has more.

Draw a line to compare.

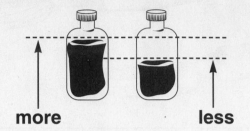

more   **less**

Circle the one that has more.

Try It • Circle the one that has more.

1.

2.

Circle the one that has about the same amount.

3.

4.

Name_____

Power Practice • Circle the one that has more.

5.

6.

7.

8.

9.

10.

Circle the one that has about the same amount.

11.

12.

13.

14.

15.

16.

More or Less

Learn

Find the side that is up.

More goes down.

Less goes up.

What Can I Do?
I want to find the side that has less.

Circle the side that has less.

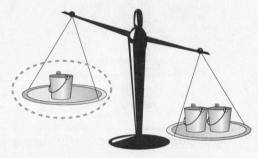

I [ ] is less than 2 [ ] .

Try It • Circle the side that has less.

1.

2.

Power Practice • Circle the side that has less.

3.

4.

Heavier or Lighter

Learn

What Can I Do?
I want to find the one that is heavier.

Find the one that is heavier.

heavier   lighter

Circle the one that is heavier.

Try It • Circle the one that is heavier.

1.

2.

Power Practice • Circle the one that is heavier.

3.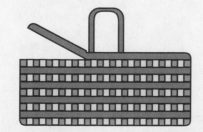

4.

The Long and the Short of It

Draw something in real life that is longer.

1. Longer than a  .

2. Longer than a  .

Draw something in real life that is shorter.

3. Shorter than a .   **4.** Shorter than a .

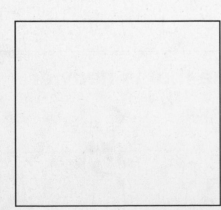

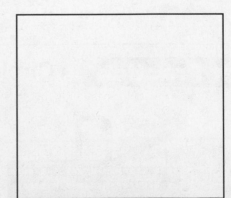

Heavy Duty

Put the things in order from lightest to heaviest. Write the letters on the lines to show the order.

I.    

S   A   N

_____   _____   _____

2.   

M   E   L

_____   _____   _____

3.       

T   C   L

_____   _____   _____

Circle the letters of the lightest and heaviest things in each row. Read down the letters of the lightest things. Read down the letters of the heaviest things. Write the message here.

____ ____ ____ ____ ____ ____

Spatial Order

Learn

Find the shape inside the box.

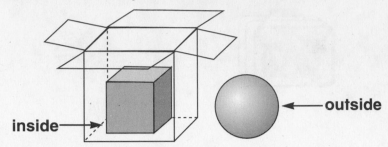

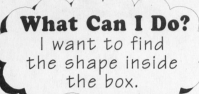

What Can I Do?
I want to find the shape inside the box.

Circle the shape that is inside the box.

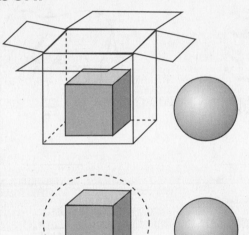

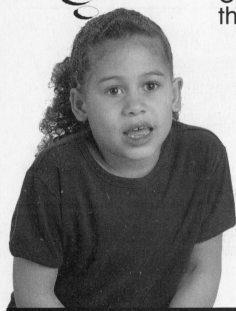

Try It • **Circle each shape.**

1. Outside the box

2. Inside the box

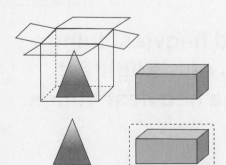

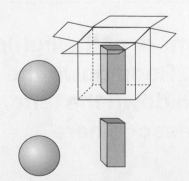

Name_____

Power Practice • Circle each shape.

3. Inside the box

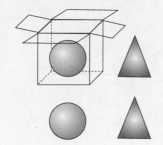

4. Outside the box

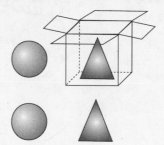

5. Inside the box

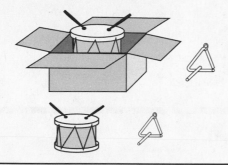

6. Outside the box

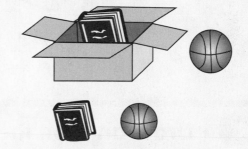

7. Inside the box

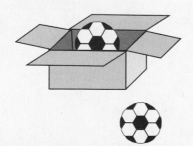

8. Outside the box

9. Outside the box

10. Inside the box

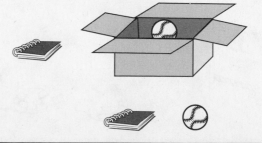

Follow Directions

Learn

Name each place.

first second third fourth fifth

Draw an X on the fifth one.

Try It • **Draw an X on the animal.**

1. Draw an X on the third animal.

first second third fourth fifth

---

2. Draw an X on the second animal.

Power Practice • Draw an X on the animal.

3. Draw an X on the first animal.

4. Draw an X on the second animal.

5. Draw an X on the fifth animal.

6. Draw an X on the fourth animal.

Sort by Shape: Shapes That Roll

Learn

Shapes that roll are round.

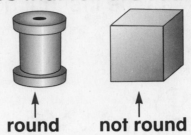

round   not round

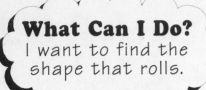

What Can I Do?
I want to find the shape that rolls.

Shapes that roll have no corners.

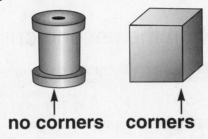

no corners   corners

Circle the shape that rolls.

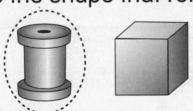

Try It • Circle the one that rolls.

1.

2.

3.

4.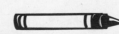

Power Practice • Circle the one that rolls.

5.

6.

7.

8.

9.

10.

Circle the one that does not roll.

11.

12.

13.

14.

Sort by Shape: Same Shape

Learn

What Can I Do?
I want to find shapes that are the same.

Find the shapes that match.

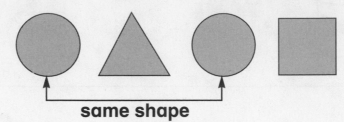

same shape

Circle the shapes that are the same.

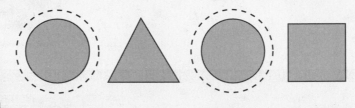

Try It • Circle the shapes that are the same.

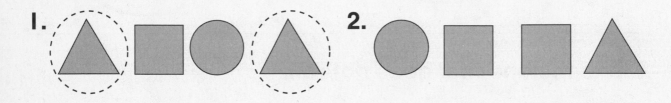

1.

2.

3.

4.

5.

6.

Name________________________________

Power Practice • **Circle the shapes that are the same.**

7.

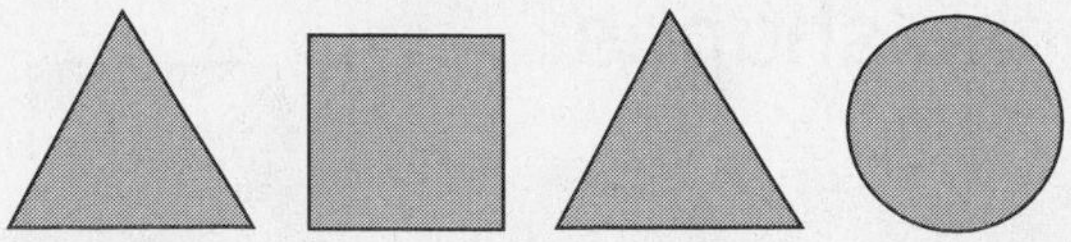

8.

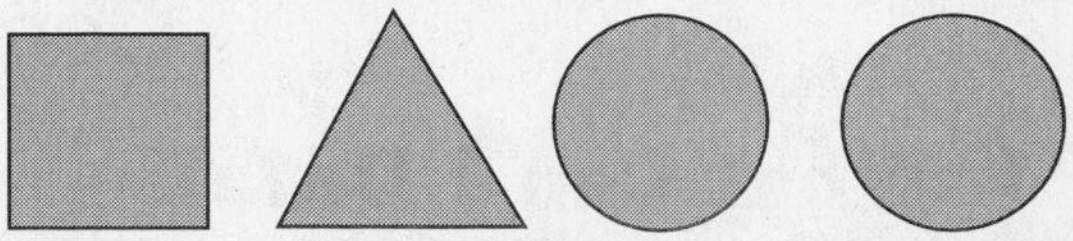

9.

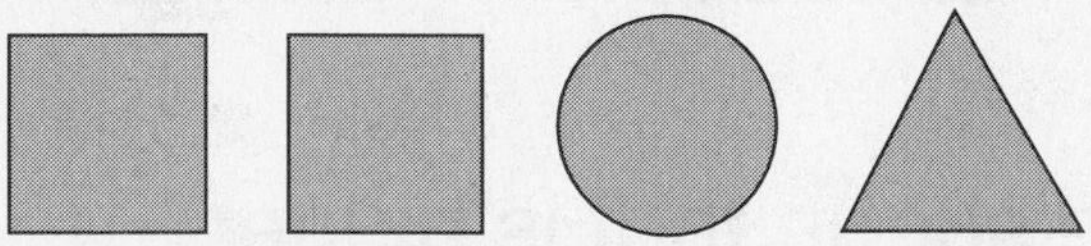

10.

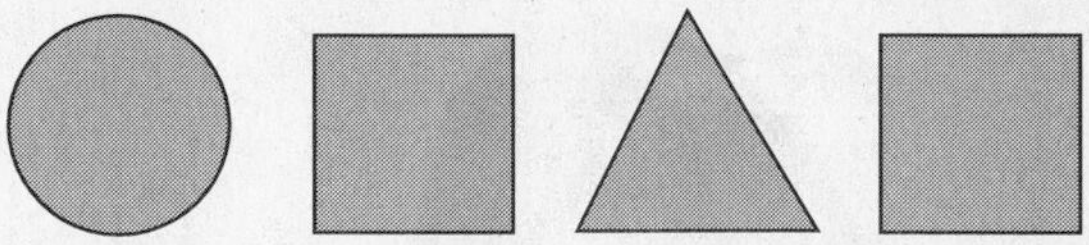

11.

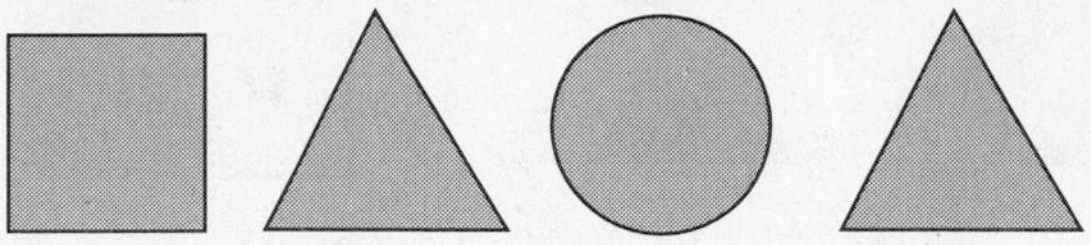

12.

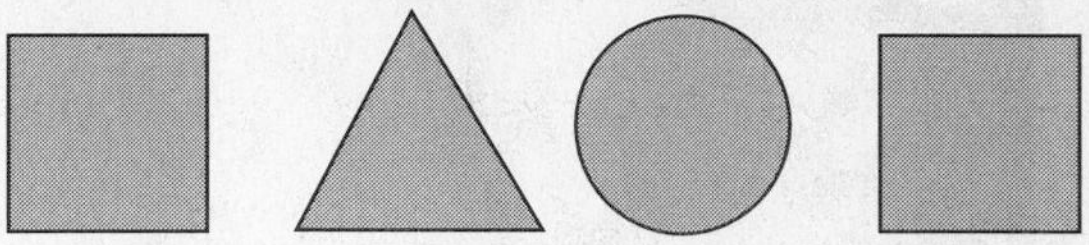

13.

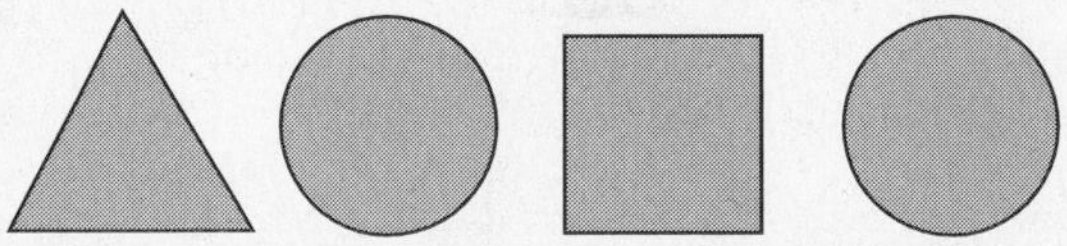

14.

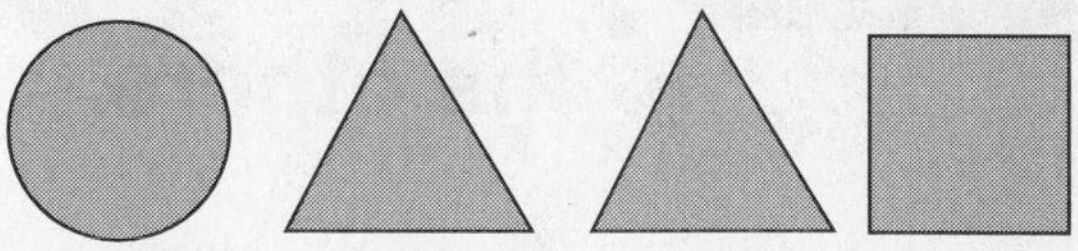

15.

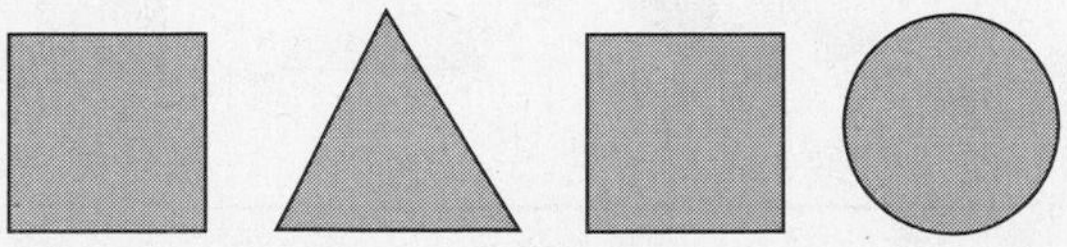

16.

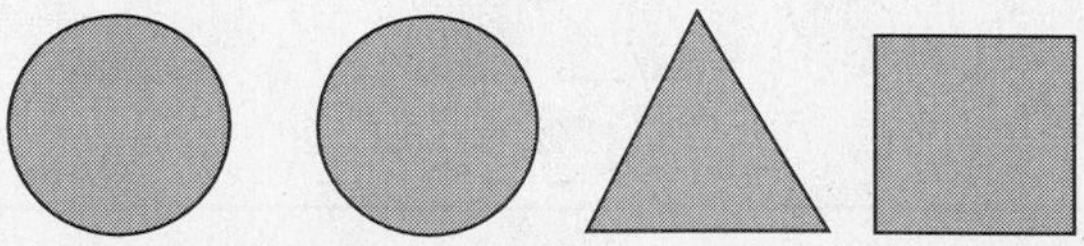

17.

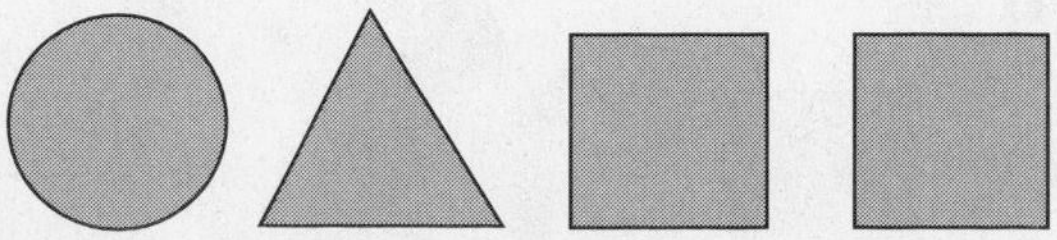

18.

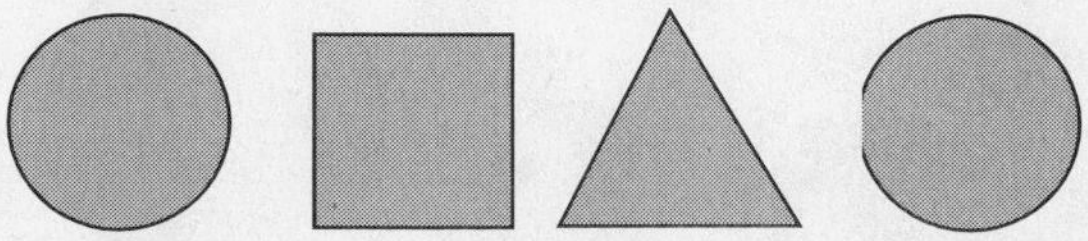

Sort by Size

Learn

Compare the shapes.

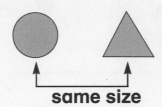

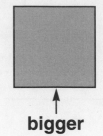

same size   bigger

What Can I Do?
I want to find the shape that is bigger.

Circle the shape that is bigger.

Try It . Circle the shape that is bigger than the others.

1.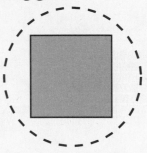

2. 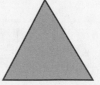 triangle square

Circle the shapes that are the same size.

3.

4.

Power Practice . Circle the shape that is bigger than the others.

5.

6.

7.

8.

9.

10.

Circle the shapes that are the same size.

11.

12.

13.

14.

15.

16.

Name_____

The Same-Shape Game

Cut out the cards. Mix them up. Put them face down in a pile. Play with a partner.

To play:
Take turns. Take a card. Move your to the next space with that shape.

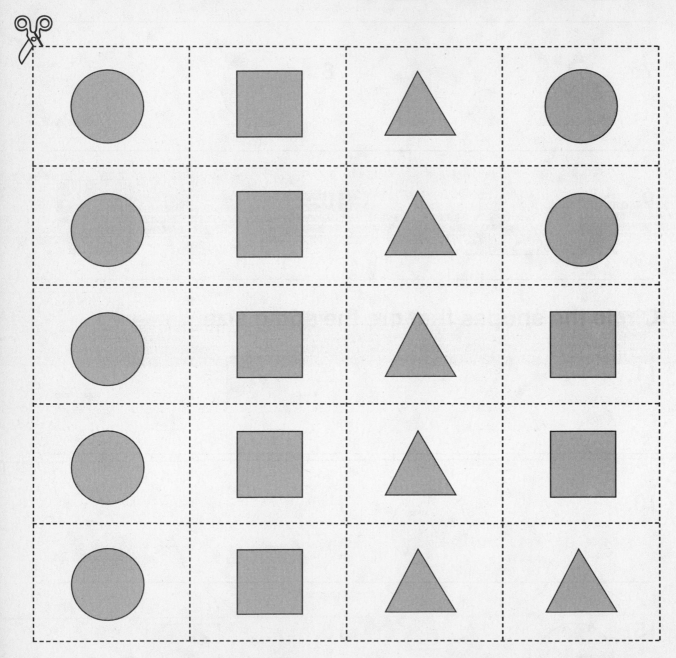

The Same-Shape Game

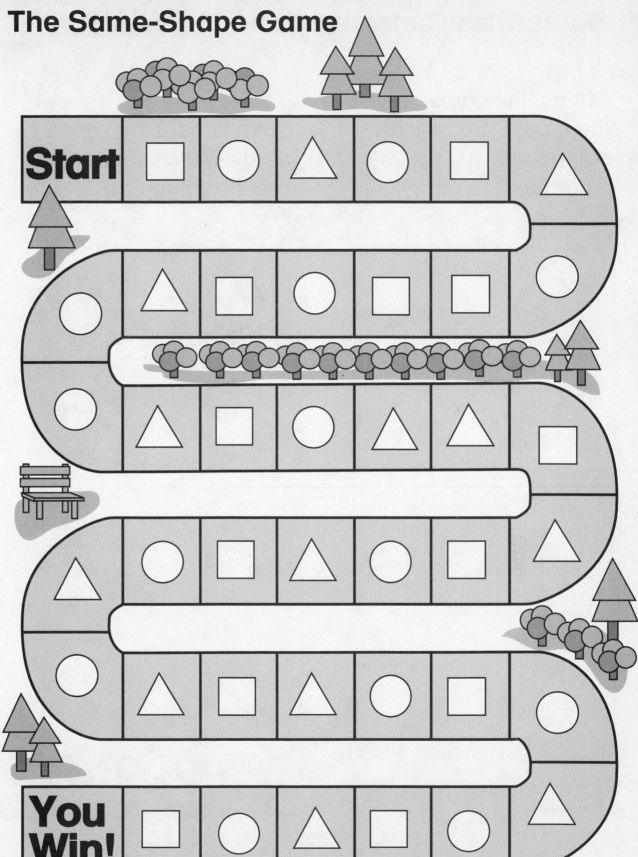

Same-Size Concentration

Cut out the cards. Mix them up. Spread them out facedown. Play with a partner.

To Play:
Take turns. Turn over 2 cards. Match shapes that are the same size.

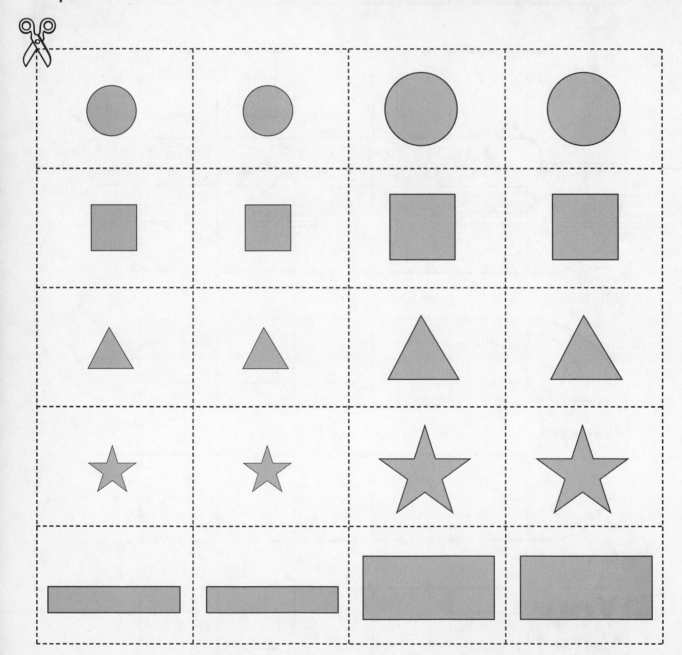

Shape Detective

Read the clues.
Circle the shape that matches each clue.

I. I am the second big ▲.

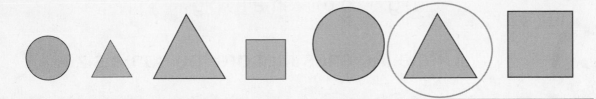

2. I am the first big ●.

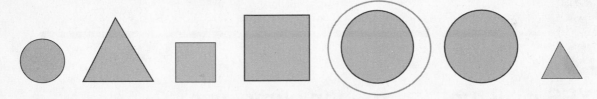

3. I am the first small ■.

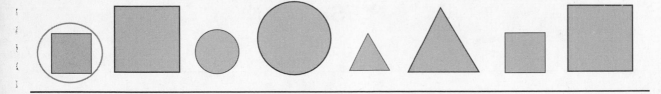

4. I am the last big ■.

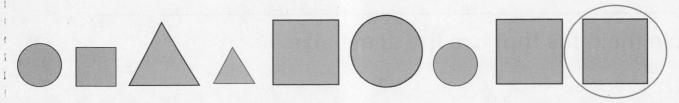

© McGraw-Hill School Division

Name_____

Sort by Size

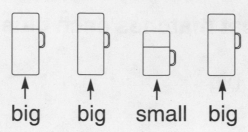
I want to find the objects that are the same size.

Compare the sizes.

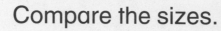

big   big   small   big

Circle the ones that are the same size.

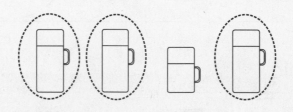

Try It

Circle **YES** if all the are the same size.

Circle **NO** if they are not all the same size.

1.   **YES**   (**NO**)

2.   **YES**   **NO**

Circle the ones that are the same size

3.   4.

Name_____

Circle YES if all the ☕ are the same size. Circle NO if they are not all the same size.

5. 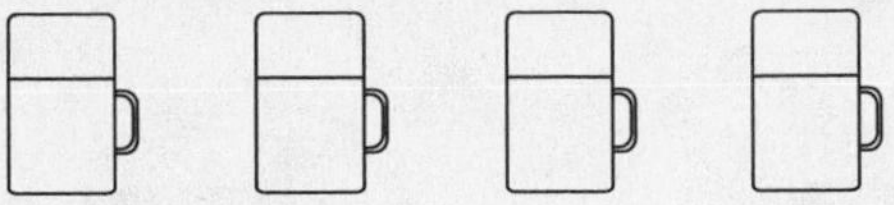 YES   NO

6. 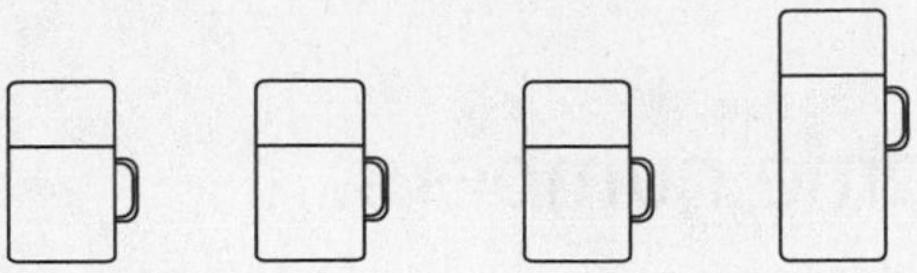 YES   NO

7. 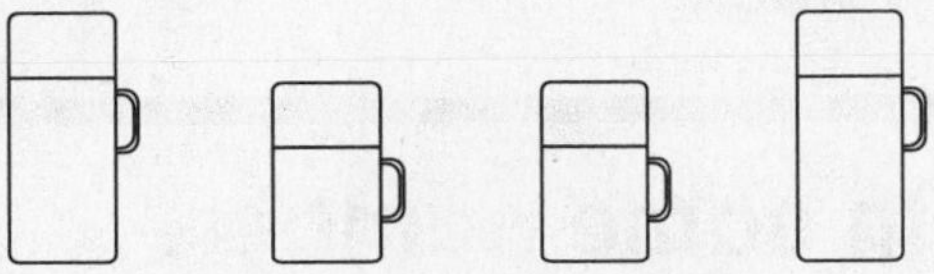 YES   NO

Circle the ones that are the same size.

8. 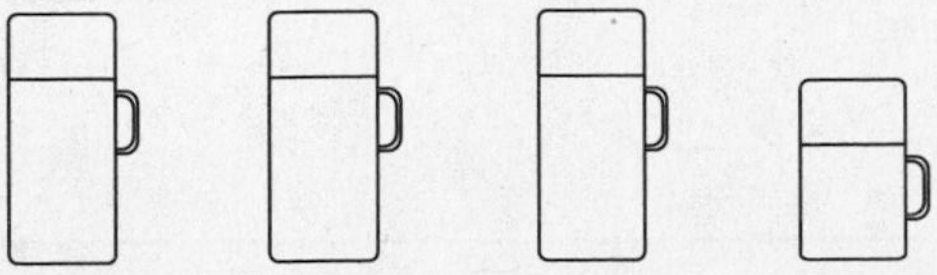   **9.**

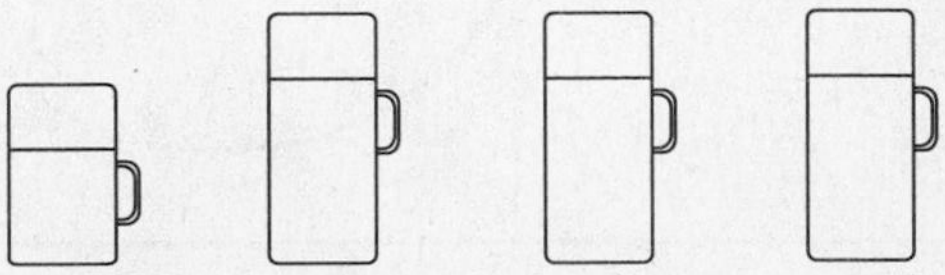

10. 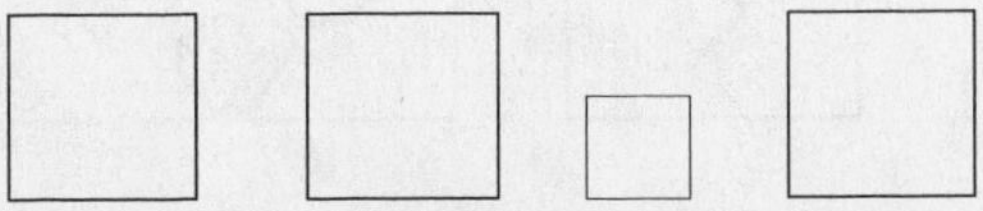   **11.**

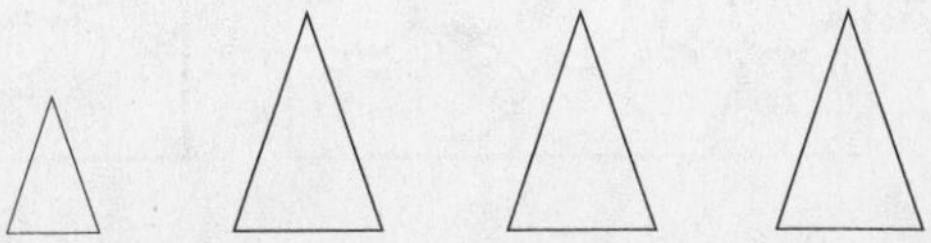

© McGraw-Hill School Division

Equal Number

Learn

Count how many.

2  3

What Can I Do?
I want to find objects that have the same number.

2   1

Circle the same numbers.

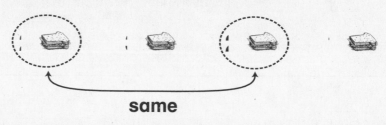

same

Try It • Circle the ones with same number.

1.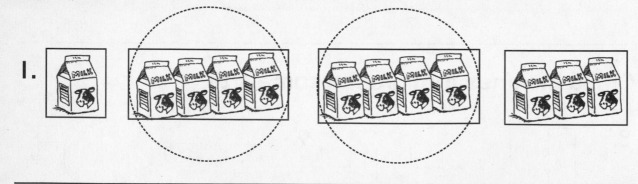

2.

Power Practice

• Circle the ones with the same number.

3.

4.

5.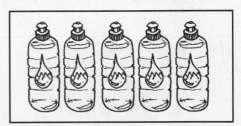

6.

7.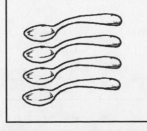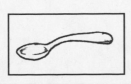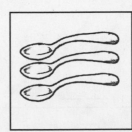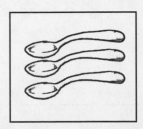

Count to 10

Learn

What Can I Do?
I want to count.

Count how many.

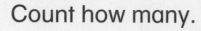

1   2   3   4   5

6   7   8   9   10

Write how many.

<u>10</u>

Try It • Write how many.

1.

_____

2.

_____

3.

_____

4.

_____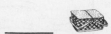

Name_____

Power Practice • Write how many.

5.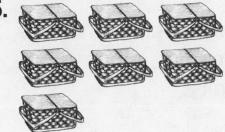

_____

6.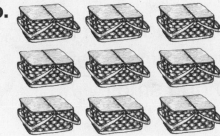

_____

7.

_____

8.

_____

9.

_____

10.

_____

11.

_____

12.

_____

Design a Beach Blanket

Draw the shapes on each beach blanket.

1. Draw a design that has the same number of big ◯ and small ◯.

2. Draw a design that has more big △ than small △.

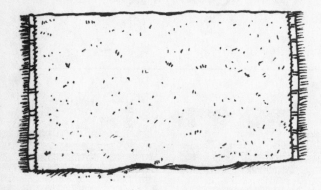

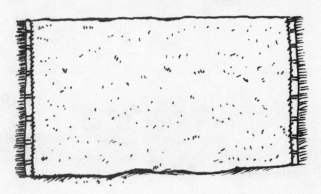

3. Draw a design that has the same number of big △ and small ☐.

4. Draw a design that has fewer small △ than big ◯.

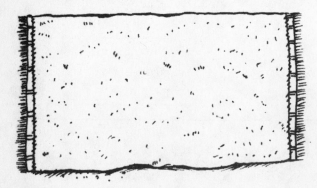

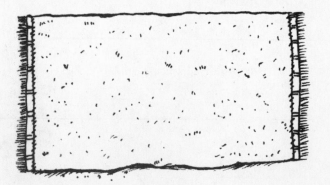

Name_____

Domino Fun

Cut out the dominoes.
Mix them up. Put them
facedown in a pile.
Play with a partner.

To play:
Take turns. Turn over 2 [:|:] to start. Turn over 1 [:|:] from the pile. Match the dots at one end to one of your [:|:]. If you have no match, take a [:|:].

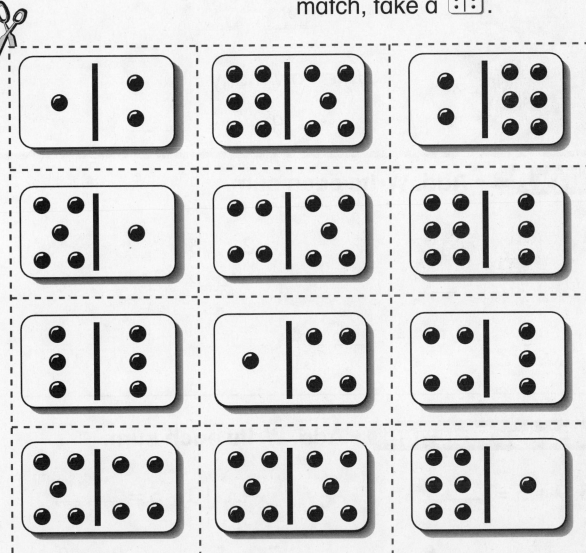

Add Sums to 20

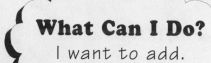 **Learn**

 What Can I Do?
I want to add.

$$4 + 6 = \underline{}$$

Put the groups together to add.

Count how many.

Write how many.

$$4 + 6 = \underline{10}$$ 🌼

Try It • Add. Write each sum.

1.

$$3 + 5 = \underline{8}$$ 🌼

2. $\begin{array}{r} 8 \\ + 5 \\ \hline \end{array}$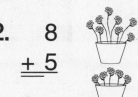

Power Practice • Add. Write each sum.

3. $9 + 5 = \underline{}$

4. $10 + 5 = \underline{}$

5. $\begin{array}{r} 7 \\ + 4 \\ \hline \end{array}$

6. $\begin{array}{r} 9 \\ + 7 \\ \hline \end{array}$

7. $\begin{array}{r} 5 \\ + 7 \\ \hline \end{array}$

8. $\begin{array}{r} 8 \\ + 6 \\ \hline \end{array}$

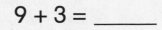
Add Sums to 20: Counting On

Learn

What Can I Do?
I want to count on to add.

$9 + 3 =$ _____

Count on to add.

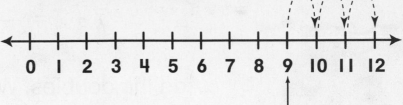

0 1 2 3 4 5 6 7 8 9 10 11 12

Count: 9-10-11-12

$9 + 3 = \underline{12}$

Try It • Count on to add. Write each sum.

1. $8 + 3 = \underline{11}$

2. $\begin{array}{r} 10 \\ +\ 2 \\ \hline \end{array}$

3. $\begin{array}{r} 9 \\ +\ 1 \\ \hline \end{array}$

Power Practice • Count on to add. Write each sum.

4. $7 + 2 =$ _____

5. $6 + 3 =$ _____

---

6. $\begin{array}{r} 5 \\ +\ 1 \\ \hline \end{array}$

7. $\begin{array}{r} 8 \\ +\ 2 \\ \hline \end{array}$

8. $\begin{array}{r} 7 \\ +\ 3 \\ \hline \end{array}$

9. $\begin{array}{r} 10 \\ +\ 1 \\ \hline \end{array}$

Add Sums to 20: Doubles

Learn

What Can I Do?
I want to add doubles.

$7 + 7 = $ ——

Add the doubles. Write the sum.

$7 + 7 = \underline{14}$

Try It • Add the doubles. Write the sum.

1.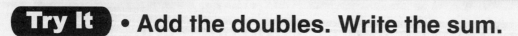

$5 + 5 = \underline{10}$

2. $\begin{array}{r} 3 \\ + 3 \\ \hline \end{array}$

Power Practice • Add the doubles. Write the sum.

3. $9 + 9 = $ ——

4. $6 + 6 = $ ——

5. $\begin{array}{r} 8 \\ + 8 \\ \hline \end{array}$

6. $\begin{array}{r} 4 \\ + 4 \\ \hline \end{array}$

7. $\begin{array}{r} 10 \\ + 10 \\ \hline \end{array}$

8. $\begin{array}{r} 2 \\ + 2 \\ \hline \end{array}$

Add Sums to 20: Doubles + 1

Learn

What Can I Do?
I want to add doubles plus 1.

$8 + 9 =$ _____

Find a near double. Write the sum.

$8 + 8 = 16$

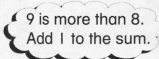
9 is more than 8.
Add 1 to the sum.

$8 + 9 =$ __17__

Try It • Add. Write each sum.

1.

   $6 + 5 =$ __11__

2. $\begin{array}{r} 8 \\ +7 \\ \hline \end{array}$

Power Practice • Add. Write each sum.

3. $4 + 5 =$ _____   4. $6 + 7 =$ _____

5. $\begin{array}{r} 3 \\ +2 \\ \hline \end{array}$ 6. $\begin{array}{r} 10 \\ +9 \\ \hline \end{array}$ 7. $\begin{array}{r} 4 \\ +3 \\ \hline \end{array}$ 8. $\begin{array}{r} 5 \\ +6 \\ \hline \end{array}$

Count to 100

Learn

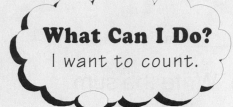

What Can I Do?
I want to count.

Write how many tens.

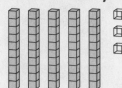

__5__ tens _____ ones = _____

Write how many ones.

__5__ tens __3__ ones = _____

Write how many.

__5__ tens __3__ ones = __53__

Try It • **Write the number of tens and ones.
Then write the number.**

1.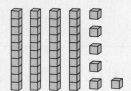

__4__ tens __6__ ones = __46__

2.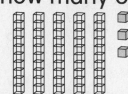

_____ tens _____ ones = _____

3.

_____ tens _____ ones = _____

4.

_____ ten _____ ones = _____

Name_____

Power Practice • Write the numbers of tens and ones. Then write the number.

5. _____ tens _____ ones = _____

6. _____ tens _____ ones = _____

7. _____ tens _____ ones = _____

8. _____ tens _____ ones = _____

9. _____ tens _____ ones = _____

10. _____ tens _____ ones = _____

11. _____ tens _____ one = _____

12. _____ ten _____ ones = _____

13. _____ tens _____ ones = _____

14. _____ tens _____ ones = _____

Names for Numbers

Learn

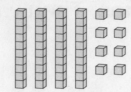

48 = 4 tens 8 ones.

Trade 1 ten for 10 ones

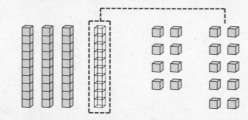

Count the tens and ones.

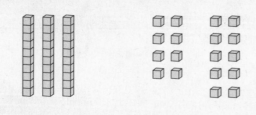

What Can I Do?

I want to show the number another way.

48 = __3__ tens __18__ ones

Try It • Circle the model that shows another way to name the number.

1. 24 ones

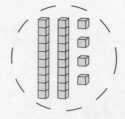

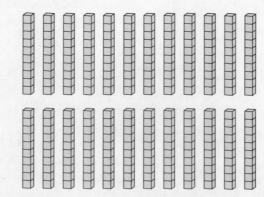

2 tens 4 ones   24 tens

Name_____

2. 4 tens 3 ones

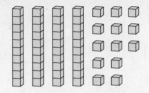

4 tens 13 ones   3 tens 13 ones

Power Practice • **Circle the model that shows another way to name the number.**

3. 15 ones

1 ten 5 ones   1 ten 15 ones

---

4. 18 ones

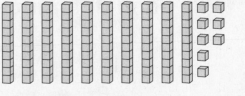

10 tens 8 ones   1 ten 8 ones

---

5. 5 tens 4 ones

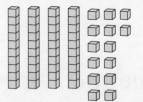

4 tens 14 ones   5 tens 14 ones

---

6. 6 tens 0 ones

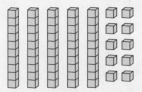

5 tens 10 ones   5 tens 1 one

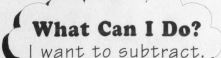
Subtract from 20

Learn

What Can I Do?
I want to subtract.

$17 - 7 =$ _____ ✿

Cross out to subtract.

Write how many are left.

$17 - 7 =$ _10_ ✿

Try It • Subtract. Write each difference.

1. ✿ ✿ ✿ ✿ ✿
   ✿ ✿

   $7 - 5 =$ _2_

2. 12 ✿ ✿ ✿ ✿
   − 8 ✿ ✿ ✿ ✿
        ✿ ✿ ✿ ✿

Power Practice • Subtract. Write each difference.

3. $16 - 9 =$ _____

4. $13 - 5 =$ _____

5. 11
   − 8

6. 17
   − 8

7. 19
   − 9

8. 15
   − 6

Subtract: Counting Back

Learn

What Can I Do?
I want to count back to subtract.

$11 - 3 = $ _____

Count back to subtract.

0 1 2 3 4 5 6 7 8 9 10 11 12

Count back 3: 11 - 10 - 9 - 8

$11 - 3 = $ _8_

Try It • Count back to subtract. Write the difference.

1. $10 - 2 = $ _8_   **2.** $9 - 1 = $ _____

Power Practice • Count back to subtract. Write the difference.

3. $7 - 1 = $ _____   **4.** $11 - 2 = $ _____

5. $10 - 3 = $ _____   **6.** $12 - 3 = $ _____

7. $\begin{array}{r} 6 \\ -2 \\ \hline \end{array}$ **8.** $\begin{array}{r} 12 \\ -2 \\ \hline \end{array}$ **9.** $\begin{array}{r} 8 \\ -3 \\ \hline \end{array}$ **10.** $\begin{array}{r} 11 \\ -1 \\ \hline \end{array}$

Subtract Using Doubles

Learn

What Can I Do?
I want to use
doubles to subtract.

$10 - 5 = $ ____

Think about doubles.

$10 - 5 = $ ____

$5 + 5 = 10$

Write the difference.

$10 - 5 = \underline{5}$

Try It • Subtract. Think about doubles.
Write the difference.

1. $14 - 7 = \underline{7}$ 2. $8 - 4 = \underline{4}$

Power Practice • Subtract. Write the difference.

3. $4 - 2 = $ ____   4. $2 - 1 = $ ____

5. $18 - 9 = $ ____   6. $12 - 6 = $ ____

7. $\begin{array}{r} 16 \\ -\ 8 \\ \hline \end{array}$ 8. $\begin{array}{r} 20 \\ -10 \\ \hline \end{array}$ 9. $\begin{array}{r} 6 \\ -3 \\ \hline \end{array}$ 10. $\begin{array}{r} 10 \\ -\ 5 \\ \hline \end{array}$

Subtract Related Facts

Learn

What Can I Do?
I want to subtract related facts.

Subtract.

❁ ❁ ❁ ❁ ❁
❁ ❁ ❁

8 − 5 = _____ ❁

8 − 3 = _____ ❁

Look for related facts.

8 − 5 = __3__ ❁

8 − 3 = __5__ ❁

Try It • **Subtract.**

1. ❁ ❁ ❁ ❁
   ❁ ❁ ❁

   7 − 3 = __4__

   7 − 4 = __3__

2. 9   9   ❁ ❁ ❁ ❁ ❁ ❁
   −3   −6   ❁ ❁ ❁

Power Practice • **Subtract.**

3. 12 − 9 = _____   4. 13 − 6 = _____

   12 − 3 = _____   13 − 7 = _____

---

7.   8   8   6.   11   11   7.   15   15
    −6   −2   −4   −7   −8   −7

Number Names

Write each number. Then write it in the correct box on the number line below.

1. 2 tens 10 ones = _____   **2.** I ten II ones = _____

_____

3. 2 tens 13 ones = _____   **4.** I ten 25 ones = _____

_____

5. I5 ones = _____   **6.** I ten I6 ones = _____

_____

7. 2 tens II ones = _____   **8.** I ten 9 ones = _____

_____

9. 23 ones = _____   **10.** I ten I7 ones = _____

_____

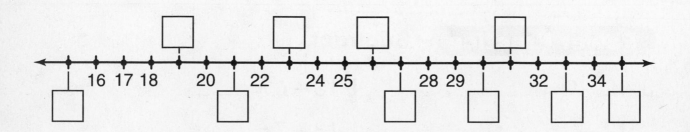

Subtraction Match

Cut out the cards . Mix them up.
Put the cards face down in a pile. Play
with a partner.

To play: Each player takes 1 card from the
pile. The player with the greater difference
takes both cards. If the differences are the
same, the winner of the next round takes
all 4 cards.

20 – 10	14 – 17	14 – 9	9 – 7
18 – 9	12 – 5	13 – 9	11 – 9
16 – 7	12 – 6	6 – 2	7 – 6
16 – 8	14 – 8	10 – 7	10 – 9
18 – 10	10 – 5	11 – 8	12 – 2